MG T-SERIES

THE COMPLETE STORY

Other Titles in the Crowood AutoClassics Series

T-SERIES

THE COMPLETE STORY

Graham Robson

The Crowood Press

First published in 1998 by
The Crowood Press Ltd
Ramsbury, Marlborough
Wiltshire SN8 2HR

www.crowood.com

Paperback edition 2007

This impression 2014

British Library Cataloguing-in-Publication Data
A catalogue record for this book is available from the British Library.

ISBN 978 1 86126 909 6

Typeface used: New Century Schoolbook.

Printed and bound in India by Replika Press Pvt. Ltd.

Contents

Acknowledgements

As always, I couldn't possibly have completed this book without the help of many friends, colleagues and MG enthusiasts.

Over the years that I have been writing about cars, and about MGs, many people in what we now call the Rover Group have helped me, with facts, figures, advice, and support. Nowadays, at the British Motor Industry Heritage Trust at Gaydon, Anders Clausager (Archivist) and his colleagues have been a continuing source of historic material and statistics. More recently, I was helped by other MG enthusiasts, including Malcolm Green of Magna Press, David Knowles and Peter Browning. Last, but by no means least, an interview with Jack Daniels, whose design career began at MG in the 1920s, was fascinating, and informative.

Without them, it simply couldn't have been done.

Graham Robson

Introduction

The first car I ever saw competing in a rally was an MG TD Midget. The first car I ever bought was an MG TA. Probably the first car I ever saw pictured in a children's motoring book was an MG sports car. Is it any wonder that I have always been an avid follower of MG, and in particular of the T-series cars?

There are so many reasons why MG's long-running T-Series cars were of lasting importance to sports car fans all around the world. I'd go so far as to state that without these MGs, and what they achieved, there might never have been a British sports car industry, and certainly not a British sports car tradition.

It was the 1930s-style Abingdon-built MGs, more than any other make or model of car, which made sports car motoring available to thousands, instead of dozens, of people; to the man in the street rather than the well-to-do. The T-Series, new in 1936, carried that process forward another stage.

It was the TC which started the flood of MG exports to the USA in the 1940s, and it was the TD which turned MG into a real sports car best-seller on that continent in the 1950s. It was, above all, the T-Series cars which laid all the foundations, and the MG reputation, for the MGAs, MGBs and 1960s-generation Midgets which followed.

Well before this book was written, most of the factual information about the T-Series – where and when they were built, what was the basis of their engineering,

and how many cars went to whichever markets – was well known. Although these facts are re-stated here, of course, I have also tried to fill in the 'whys' and 'hows' of this long-running pedigree.

Because of the long period in which T-Series cars were the mainstay of Abingdon's production lines, this makes a fascinating story. There were many outside influences, the most important of these being the rationalization of Nuffield, the Second World War, the lack of investment granted to Abingdon, the need to export most of the output, the Austin-Healey 100 and the foundation of BMC. I have tried to make it clear where each fitted in.

It is also important to make clear that only you – the independent traders, the enthusiasts and the MG owners – have been able to keep T-Series cars on the road in recent years, for there has been no long-term encouragement from MG's proprietors. One reason for this is that the company changed hands so often in the 1960s and 1970s that all continuity was lost. It was commercial insight, rather than a love of the marque, which brought MG sports cars back into existence in the 1990s.

This book, therefore, is a celebration of MG and the MG sports car as it was – not as it is. It is a celebration of interesting cars, great characters and – not least – of the clubs and other organizations which have kept so many of the cars on the roads for more than 50 years after production ended.

Evolution

Date	Event
1928	First-ever MG Midget, the M-Type, introduced.
1929	MG assembly moved into a factory at Abingdon.
1935	Ownership of MG transferred from Lord Nuffield (personal ownership) to Morris Motors, itself the manufacturing arm of the new Nuffield Organisation. All design activities were transferred from Abingdon to Cowley.
June 1936	TA model introduced.
May 1939	TB model replaced TA.
September/ October 1939	MG private car production suspended, in favour of war work. TB model discontinued.
November 1945	TC model introduced, effectively an up-dated TB.
May 1947	Introduction of YA saloon, with new-type independent front suspension and chassis frame. The TD of 1950 would be developed from this design.
November 1949	TC model discontinued. TD production began (with announcement in January 1950).
October 1953	TF model introduced, as a direct replacement for the TD.
Autumn 1954	First production of TF1500 models, to replace the original type TF.
April 1955	TF1500 assembly officially ended, though no announcement was made at this time.
June 1955	MGA prototypes raced in the Le Mans Twenty-Four Hour race.
September 1955	Introduction of the MGA road car, bringing the T-Series era officially to a close.

1 Safety Fast: The Abingdon Touch

As everyone surely knows, MG was Cecil Kimber's idea, and his boss William Morris, as general manager of Morris Garages in Oxford in 1922, gave him a free hand. Just so long as the business was making money, Morris – busy with the expansion of his car-making empire at Cowley – was not inclined to interfere. For Kimber, who was not only a capable manager but a motoring enthusiast too, this was almost an open invitation to develop his own enterprise. Starting by commissioning special-bodied 'bullnose' Morris models for sale to Morris Garages customers, it was only a short step for him to badge them up as MGs – M.G. (still with full stops after the initials at this time) being an acronym for Morris Garages – and the now-famous marque evolved from there. Most historians currently agree that the very first MG-badged cars appeared in 1923, using modified Morris Cowley chassis, and with two-seater tourer body styles by Raworth (a small Oxford-based coachbuilder). Bigger, better, faster and more expensive MGs then followed in the mid-1920s, the fledgling company being moved frenetically from factory to factory to find enough space.

The real breakthrough, and the launch of the car which turned MG into an international sports car icon, came in 1928. Once again basing an MG on easily

Cecil Kimber conceived the very first MG sports cars in the mid-1920s, and ran the MG Car Company until 1941, when he was brutally sacked.

William Morris (who became Lord Nuffield) hired Cecil Kimber to run Morris Garages in the early 1920s, then encouraged him to build up MG; however, he rarely showed much interest in the sports-car legends which resulted. When Len Lord imposed his own will on MG in 1935, Lord Nuffield stood by and let it happen. Many MG enthusiasts never forgave him for that.

Cecil Kimber at the wheel of 'Old Number One', the trials special built for him in 1925, and a car which he once affectionately described as the first real MG. But it wasn't...

adaptable Morris Motors engineering, Kimber invented the very first Midget. From 1929 – and particularly after MG moved to its definitive home at Abingdon – the long-running family of Midgets was born.

ADOLESCENCE

The model name 'Midget' told its own story. Compared with previous MGs, particularly the six-cylinder 18/80 which was introduced ahead of the same Olympia Motor Show, this was a much smaller, much cheaper and potentially much more saleable model. As regards price, it is important to make a critical point. For 1929 the existing 14/40 Mk IV Tourer model was priced at £335, and the new 18/80 cost £480. The tiny 847cc-engined M-Type Midget, on the other hand, was labelled at a mere £175, and no rival (really, there were no rivals) could approach that.

For MG and Kimber, therefore, everything came together at the right time. First there was the development of the low-priced M-Type Midget; second, there was the move to Abingdon; and third, there was the growing realization among sporting drivers that here, at last, was a two-seater they could afford. Fortunately for Kimber and MG, the move to Abingdon came just in time, because it would have been impossible to have satisfied the demand for Midgets from the existing overcrowded building in Edmund Road, Cowley. Once the move had been completed, production soared: only 300 MGs were built at Edmund Road in 1928, but no fewer than 1,850 cars left Abingdon in 1930.

I cannot stress the importance of the M-Type Midget too highly, for it set up the templates of all MG sports cars built until

Most early MG production cars looked like this 14/28 model of 1925. These were quite large and heavy cars, which pre-dated the Midget pedigree by several years.

the end of the 1940s, including the TA, TB and TC models. Like later cars, the M-Type featured:

- a simple, ladder-style chassis frame, with channel-section side members and little cross bracing;
- beam front and rear axles, suspended on rock-hard, half-elliptic leaf springs,with lever-arm dampers;
- a neat and totally characteristic two-seater body style, with the vertical radiator crowned by the MG octagon badge which everyone recognized;
- a bench seat, a central gearchange, and a handbrake alongside the transmission tunnel;

- simple body construction, based on a wooden frame with pressed or folded panels attached to that skeleton;
- engine-bay access by two fold-up panels, hinged along the centre line of the car;
- exposed headlamps, close to the vertical radiator;
- wire spoke wheels.

Although it wasn't a very quick car – with no more than about 20bhp on early models, it struggled to reach a top speed of 60mph (97kmph) – it had enormous character, which always endeared it to road testers. No doubt *The Autocar* could be expected to think well of any new British

MG assembly moved to the Pavlova Works at Abingdon in 1929/1930, originally using the buildings closest to the aerial camera, which is facing northwards. Much expansion would follow in the next half-century. Note the separate three-storey administration building just to the north of the production buildings. Today's MG Car Club HQ is a little further along that road.

car at this time, but even so, its road test, published in June 1939, was headlined: 'An Extraordinarily Fascinating Little Car: Comfort at Speed'. The main test began with the words: 'Not only has the MG Midget a fascinating appearance, but it goes so exceedingly well. Sixty to sixty-five miles an hour with it are not adventure but delight. It sits down on the road like a thoroughbred, and at high speed feels more like a big car than a tiny one...'

That was the effect, too, that the early Midgets had on the customers, and MG prospered on the strength of this; moreover later Midgets – bigger, faster, and more flamboyantly styled and equipped, though still remarkably low-priced – would build on it, too. Even though the M-Type's Wolseley-based overhead-camshaft engine (like the entire chassis, this was lifted from the Morris Minor) was a most unfortunate size

for racing purposes – at 847cc it sat awkwardly in the middle of the 751cc to 1,000cc racing category – it proved to be remarkably tuneable, which is why design and development engineer Hubert Charles now enters my story. As John Thornley later wrote in *Maintaining the Breed*, Charles: '...gave his attention to the tuning of the Midget', and until he was rather brutally side-lined from MG design in the late 1930s, he would always be central to Midget and other MG developments.

OVERHEAD-CAM EXCELLENCE

At this point I should point out the growing link – both technical and commercial – between Cecil Kimber, MG, and Wolseley. Wolseley of Birmingham had been rescued

Simple is efficient: the very first of the famous MG Midgets, the M-Type of 1928, which was closely based on the rolling chassis of the overhead-cam-engined Morris Minor. Most of the wooden-framed body on this car was fabric-covered.

Cecil Kimber (1888 – 1945)

For nearly twenty years, between 1923 and 1941, Cecil Kimber was MG, and for many years after that his influence at Abingdon, his legacy, was ever-present. Almost single-handedly, and often with no more than amused tolerance – sometimes blind neglect – from his proprietor, Lord Nuffield, Cecil Kimber invented the MG marque and developed it from being merely a type of special-bodied 'bullnose' Morris, at the same time turning MG itself into a maker of specially engineered sports cars. He was already thirty-four years old before that famous MG-ancestor 'Old Number One' was even built – yet he was only fifty-three when Nuffield's vice chairman, Miles Thomas, sacked him at a moment's notice in 1941.

The Kimber family had originally made its money developing a printing ink business, which Cecil joined on his sixteenth birthday. While working for his family company, his right leg was badly smashed up in a road accident, and for the next couple of years he had to hobble around on crutches; he pulled through, battered but undefeated, but was left with a permanent limp. He could not fight in World War I, but took a job with Sheffield-Simplex, a prestigious car-making concern in Sheffield. It wasn't long before he moved to AC in Thames Ditton; and soon he was off again, to become works manager of Wrigley Ltd, a Birmingham-based axle and chassis parts builder. In 1921 Wrigley's finances drooped, and Kimber found himself looking for employment.

This is where fate stepped in. William Morris needed someone to run his existing retail operation, Morris Garages of Oxford; Kimber – small, hyperactive and full of energy – was hired, and was soon effectively running the business. He was always a complex character; to quote Harold Hastings of *The Motor*:

> In some ways he was quite ruthless and uncompromising, but in others he showed a very kindly streak. Above all he had enormous enthusiasm, and this, I think, produced the uncompromising ruthlessness which could make him a distinctly prickly character at times. There is no doubt that he was an idealist...

Almost immediately he turned to developing special coachwork for the Morris 'Bullnose' chassis. At first this seemed an unlikely prospect, for an early 1920s Morris chassis was distinctly uninspiring – it didn't matter how pretty the body was, there was still nothing exciting under the skin. Somehow, though, Kimber's persistence paid off, and from 1923 the very first Raworth-bodied MG went on sale. When Morris finally established the MG Car Co. Ltd at Abingdon in 1930, Kimber became the company's managing director.

After a boom-and-bust period in the early 1930s when MG's retail prices rose and sales slumped, Kimber's nemesis, Leonard Lord, came onto the scene: he told him that MG would have to change, and that henceforth Kimber would merely manage the operation for Morris Motors, he would not design the new cars. Kimber was shattered, not to say humiliated, although he did not show it. It was almost the end of his dream, for now he could only influence and advise, not generate and inspire. But in spite of this blow, this resourceful man refused to give up completely, making sure that MGs were still prominent in sporting trials and in record-breaking.

In fact he was much more involved in the TA than Lord or Nuffield ever expected, for one of its designers (H. N. Charles) had worked closely with him at Abingdon before moving to Cowley, and the two were firm friends – and much discussion had taken place in the evenings and at weekends during the preceding months...

As is detailed in the text, Kimber was forced out of Abingdon by Miles Thomas, who was Nuffield's vice chairman, and almost immediately dropped out of the limelight. His final years were a complete anti-climax: he joined Charlesworth (one-time car coachbuilders) in Coventry, then moved on to the Specialloid Piston Co. as works director. In 1945 he was tragically killed in a railway accident near London's King's Cross station.

Nothing came much smaller than the M-Type Midget, which had a 6ft 6in (1,981mm) wheelbase. Over the years the Midget would gradually grow up, the first TA being considerably roomier than this.

from receivership by William Morris, who personally paid £730,000 for the business at the end of 1926, and it was Wolseley which designed and manufactured the little overhead-cam engine for the first Morris Minor, and therefore for the M-Type Midget. Wolseley, though, had greater ambitions, which became obvious when the first of the related six-cylinder 1,271cc overhead-cam engines appeared in 1930, for the original Wolseley Hornet. Not only did 'four' and 'six' share their design philosophy, they also shared many of the machining fixtures, and components, too – for instance they used the same bore, stroke, pistons, connecting rods and valve gear. Until 1935, when MG's destiny was taken away from Cecil Kimber and thrust into the corporate hands of the Nuffield Organization, every new MG model – not merely every new Midget – was powered by one or other of those Wolseley-sourced engines.

Although MG versions became progressively more specialized, they were always recognizably derived from the Wolseley units, and always manufactured by Wolseley in Birmingham.

MG was to play 'alphabet soup' with its range of four-cylinder and six-cylinder sports cars in this period – in five years there were M, C, D, F, J, K, L, N, P, Q and R-Types – but the true ancestry of the TA was centred on just two of those models, the J2 Midgets of 1932–34, and the PA/PB Midgets of 1934–36. All of these cars progressively shared very similar styling and engineering themes, all had very similar chassis, running gear and body layouts, and all were properly impregnated with what became known as 'the Abingdon touch'. Kimber, his staff, and everyone connected with MG, were proud of what was being achieved: to a man, it seemed, they all believed that they were making the very

MG assembly at Abingdon, circa 1930, with M-Type Midgets in the background, and Mark I 18/80 cars on the nearest track. There was no sign of mechanization, for cars were all moved around by human power in those days!

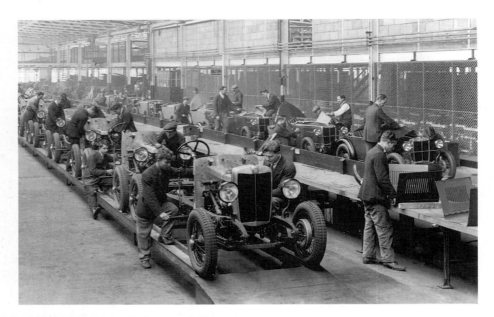

Egged on gleefully by Cecil Kimber, MG soon developed more and more complex, specialized Midgets for use in motorsport. These were C-Type 'Montlhery' Midgets being produced in a corner of Abingdon in 1931. The C-Type was the first of the Midget family to use a particular layout of chassis frame, where the side members passed under the line of the rear axle.

The famous MG radiator style had already evolved by the early 1930s when this supercharged K3 Magnette race car was built. Capt George Eyston, behind the wheel, and Count 'Johnny' Lurani shared the driving in the 1933 Mille Miglia.

best of British sports cars, and all of them believed in the company's proud slogan: 'Safety Fast'.

The J2 was really the first Midget to bring together every MG design and styling element which could later be recognized in the TA, although its graceful, swept front-wing style was not actually phased in until the autumn of 1933. Mechanically, though, the J2 had a simple ladder-style chassis, underslung at the rear, with an unsynchronized four-speed gearbox, a spiral bevel back axle, half-elliptic springs front and rear, along with lever-arm dampers. From the autumn of 1933 the definitive style had swept front wings, cutaway doors, twin scuttle humps ahead of the two passengers, and the exposed

slab tank at the rear.

Compared with the TA which was to follow, however, this was a smaller car altogether: not only did it have a 36bhp/847cc engine, but the wheelbase was only 7ft 2in (2m 18cm) and the wheeltracks just 3ft 6in (1m 6cm). By any standards, therefore, the J2 was a snug little two-seater – and either we were all smaller in the 1930s, or sports car occupants were used to being close together. Clearly, though, this was what the customer wanted, because MG had sold 3,235 M-Type Midgets, and would now follow up with 2,083 J2s in less than two full years; this was the period, however, when Kimber was never inclined to leave a good car unmolested, and in March 1934 the PA Midget took over.

The J2 Midget, produced from 1932 to 1934, was the first Midget which eventually brought together all the famous styling and engineering 'cues' which would be repeated so successfully in the TA of 1936. All the cars used a developed form of the C-Type/D-Type underslung frame; there was a slab fuel tank at the rear with a wire-spoke spare wheel fixed to it; the screen could be folded down; and the wiper motor was fixed to the top of the screen rail. The outline of the cutaway doors was a novelty for MG at the time, and the swept-wing style shown here was phased in from the autumn of 1933. For TA/TB/TC owners, this was a true ancestor, though of course it had different running gear, including the 847cc overhead-camshaft engine.

By any existing standards the PA was a delicious little machine because, urged along by Kimber, Hubert Charles and his tiny development team had looked at every aspect of the J2 – and improved it. To save time and aggravation – and, incidentally, to help with spares provisioning – some of the work which went into producing the PA was also carried over to a new six-cylinder Magnette, the NA. Although the wheel-tracks were the same as before (which meant that carryover axles and components could be specified), the chassis was sturdier and the wheelbase had been stretched by 1.3in (3.3cm), the brakes had been enlarged from 8in (20cm) to 12in (30cm) diameter, while the engine had been thoroughly reworked (it included a three-main-bearing, instead of a two-bearing crankshaft). Not only that, but the

styling – which had been finalized by building a car, rather than by spending hours in a studio and drawing shapes – was even more delicious and integrated than ever before. Except that it was still quite a small car – it was only 11ft 3in (3.4m) long – it looked even more graceful than the J2 which it supplanted.

Technically, therefore, the Midget was certainly moving with the times, but there was one major problem: that prices continued to rise. The original M-Type Midget had cost £175 (no purchase tax or VAT in those halcyon days), the first of the J2s had cost £199 10s (£199.50) in 1932, whereas the PA model cost £220. By today's end-of-the-century standards, none of these prices looks high. However, it was a fact that the PA cost twice as much as the cheapest Morris, Austin or Ford saloons, and it was also true that the PA cost 29 per cent more than the M-Type Midget had done – and this was at a time when British prices in general were actually falling slightly, and when far fewer British people could afford to run a car of any sort. Thus although the PA's specification ensured a steady demand, quite simply it was not at the same level as that achieved by the M-Type and the J2 cars, and the output of MGs from Abingdon which had peaked at 2,400 in 1932, would fall to 2,100 in 1934. Cecil Kimber thought he could trade his way out of this, for he did not see the 1934 set-back as a trend. Except for 1931, in the depth of the British financial depression, MG production had increased in every single year since the

marque was founded in 1923. MG's marketing reputation was high, and rising, the cars were becoming more and more successful in motor racing, and (along with Hubert Charles) he had great ideas for further advance in the mid-1930s.

But for Kimber, MG, and the company's on-going independence, there was already one major problem on the horizon, and his name was Leonard Lord. Newly installed at Morris Motors as Lord Nuffield's managing director, Len Lord was given a free hand to modernize, rationalize and improve his various businesses, and to do this he proposed to bring all the William Morris/Lord Nuffield enterprises together under one banner: this would be called the

Here is the true and direct Midget ancestor to the TA, this being the P-Type chassis of 1934–936, which had been designed to Cecil Kimber's requirements by Hubert Charles. Forget the fact that the PA/PB models still used the Wolseley-based overhead-camshaft engine and related transmissions, for the rest of the chassis looked like the TA which was to follow. Note, for instance, the lines of the channel-section ladder-type chassis frame, the sliding-trunnion style of leaf-spring location, and the rigid firewall between engine bay and passengers.

'Nuffield Organization'. Tacitly, if not in a 'mission statement', Len Lord was asked to do whatever was necessary to make the conglomerate more profitable, with Lord Nuffield only interfering where personal interest inspired him to do so.

SET FAIR FOR THE MID-1930s?

By 1934, as far as the outside world was concerned, Cecil Kimber's MG might have seemed well set for the next few years, even if the truth was different. Several important new models, including the PA Midget and the NA Magnette families, along with the Q-Type Midget race car, had been unveiled, and the design offices had never been busier. A new R-Type racing car, complete with independent front suspension at

front and rear, first appeared in 1935, and work also began on a new EX150 project, which was to be the largest MG yet built, a saloon, with similar all-independent suspension. Compared with 1933, although sales were struggling to keep up, trading profits in 1934 had increased considerably, to £102,984, and there was a nett surplus of nearly £21,000. For Kimber, future prospects at MG looked exciting ... except that Len Lord didn't see it that way.

Once installed as managing director of Morris Motors and given a free hand to revolutionize the business, Lord had done just that. The first candidate for change was Cowley itself, where moving assembly lines and other up-to-date production equipment ('progressive production') were installed, and after that a new range of Morris and Wolseley models (the original 'Series' cars) was set to follow.

The PB Midget of 1935/1936 was a delightful little two-seater sports car, the final development of the overhead-camshaft engine theme, with luscious styling and a very close resemblance to the TA Midget which would take over from it in 1936. Compared with the TA, though, the PB had a 6.6in (168mm) shorter wheelbase, 3in (76mm) narrower tracks, and a 43bhp/939cc engine instead of 50bhp/1,292cc. PBs were – and are – rare, for only 526 such cars were ever made. (Magna Press)

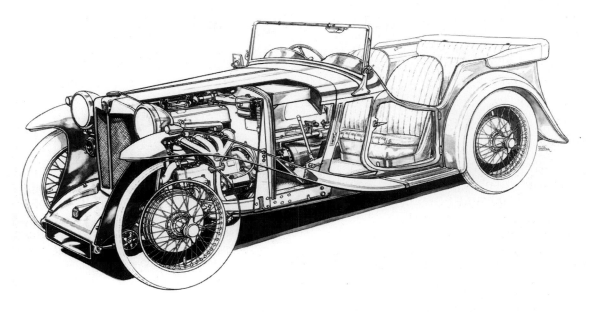

This PA cutaway drawing of a four-seater derivative shows off the layout characteristic of all MG sports cars built from the early 1930s until 1949, including the narrow-track chassis frame, the body style which obliged front-seat passengers to have legs alongside the transmission, and the instantly recognizable front-end style.

Lord then turned his attention to corporate matters: he concluded that Lord Nuffield's personal ownership of companies such as MG and Wolseley made little sense when matched to his latest financial situation (there were all manner of tax implications which had to be tested in court), and recommended that they should be 'sold' to Morris Motors. Although this is not the place to detail why and how – for further details I recommend that you read the 'official' life story, *The Life of Lord Nuffield*, by P.W.S. Andrews and Elizabeth Brunner – it could clearly have had a great effect on the MG business. Before this could happen, though, Len Lord visited Abingdon to see what Morris Motors might be acquiring from its master's back pocket; moreover his arrival was unannounced, and was received with all the panic of a fox gaining

entry to a chicken run! His philosophy could not have been more different from that of Cecil Kimber (he thought that 'works' involvement in motorsport was a waste of time, money and resources, for instance), and so there was certainly no meeting of minds. Cecil Kimber had always had the inside track in his dealings with Lord Nuffield, but at first he feared the worst since Len Lord had, after all, been given a completely free hand, and what is more, looked as if he might exercise it!

However, having studied Abingdon's balance sheets (which I analyse in more detail in the panel on page 24), we now know that Lord's first instinct was to cut out all the frills – he was certainly determined to cut out all the specialized hardware which MG, and only MG, was using. Although MG was, and always had been, a profitable

Unless you're an MG expert, it would be difficult to pick this 939cc overhead-cam-engined PB from the TA which would take over in 1936. [Magna Press]

Announced in the autumn of 1933, the 1934-model J2 was the first of the elegant swept-wing Midgets. The styling cues for the T-Series are already in place. [Magna Press]

enterprise at the operating level, it was spending so much on continual re-tooling for new models, and on marketing and publicity (motorsport was a culprit here), that its year-on-year nett profits were always in doubt. In fact it had been 'in the red' in 1931 and 1933, while in 1934 the nett profit was a mere 5 per cent of turnover.

Len Lord, who regarded profitable accounts with rather more pleasure than chequered flags and success advertising, did not like this, and his first instinct was apparently to close down MG sports car production (I wonder if he and Cecil Kimber had rubbed each other up the wrong way during his Wolseley period) in favour of building a series of much-modified Wolseleys or Morris models at the modernized Cowley factory, badging them as MGs. Persuaded otherwise (his dogmatic views could sometimes be diverted by logical argument, although it was a determined manager who would dare to try that), he agreed that MG should carry on building the P-Series Midgets and the N-Series Magnettes until successors of which he approved could be developed; but at the same time he immediately closed down the design offices, and resolved to re-establish all future MG engineering activity in the Morris Motors design office at Cowley.

Thus at a stroke, and without notice, it

Although the mid-1930s six-cylinder Magnette NB was an altogether larger car than the PA/PB types, it had very similar styling. Once again, one can see the styling details which helped to inspire the TA. [Magna Press]

seems, he killed off any future use or development of the highly specialized, Wolseley-based engines and running gear on which all existing MG models depended. There was, in fairness, a great deal of industrial logic in this, because by 1936 MG was due to be the final customer for this generation of overhead-camshaft engines – the little four-cylinder unit had been dropped by Morris (from the Minor) in 1932, and the last of the overhead-cam six-cylinder Wolseleys was due to disappear as soon as the Morris-based/Morris-engined 'Series' cars could be made ready. All of Nuffield's engine manufacturing would then be centred on a new factory in Coventry.

Because the use of that overhead-cam engine family was central to their designs, further development of the R-Type independent-suspension chassis was cancelled, and the EX150 project was killed off. Instead, to his horror, Kimber was instructed to make preparations for a new Cowley-designed, Wolseley-based MG SA '2-litre' model to go on sale in 1936. For the very

first time, it seemed, MG was being asked to assemble a car which it had not designed. From July 1935, Lord himself became managing director of MG, and although Kimber was invited to join the Morris Motors board, at Abingdon he was simultaneously demoted to become MG's general manager. For the future, Len Lord agreed that a new series of MG Midgets should be developed, but that this work would have to be done at Cowley.

Looking on from the sidelines, and always more favourably inclined to Len Lord than most of his colleagues, John Thornley noted that: 'With the 1935 takeover we thus took quite a step back, development-wise. But we became much more financially viable ... I don't think anyone ever realized the extent to which we were running into expense, as the models never ran for long enough...' From 1 July 1935, therefore, MG had to start all over again. But how long would it take to get a new car onto the market ? Was this to be a Brave New World for Abingdon?

2   TA: Cowley's First Sports Car

Most MG enthusiasts know what went into the original T-Series sports car, the TA, but not always why that actually happened. Why did the TA look like it did, and who decided its basic specification?

Even at this stage, I must point out that the TA was more about Len Lord than Cecil Kimber, as much about Robert Boyle as Hubert Charles, and more about the Morris Engines Branch than Wolseley Motors. It was, by any standards, built to a completely different 'hymn sheet' from the MG sports cars that had gone before.

Then, as now, there were so many 'whys' to be settled before T-Series design could begin. Why was the PB Midget to be dumped in favour of a much larger car? In MG terms, why was the TA to be totally different, mechanically, from any MG sports car which had preceded it? Why was this to be the first MG sports car since 1929 to be sold without an overhead camshaft engine? Why was it not to be designed at Abingdon? Len Lord, the great rationalizer (I almost wrote 'ruthless rationalizer', but I do not think he was as unthinking as that), was at

Lord Nuffield (left of the picture) and Len Lord discussing plans for the modernization of the various Morris/Nuffield businesses in the mid-1930s. Len Lord was managing director of Morris Motors Ltd at this time, and persuaded Lord Nuffield to move MG from his own personal ownership into the corporate business. At the same time he closed down both Abingdon's design offices, and the motorsport activities. It was a traumatic time for MG staff and workforce.

MG: Profits and Losses in the 1930s

Len Lord, they say, swept the MG Car Co. into the Morris Motors empire because it was losing money. Cecil Kimber, he thought, was developing the wrong sort of cars, and sales were dropping. True or false? Tall story, legend – or plain untrue ?

As ever, the detailed story isn't simple. Here's an example: certainly MG sales had slumped badly between 1932 and 1935, yet the company's gross profits reached record levels in 1934, the last year in which Cecil Kimber was in complete control. Sales then soared to a peak in 1937 (two years after Morris Motors took control), yet in that year gross profits were only 32 per cent higher than in 1934. In 1934, MG made a nett profit of £10 per car, whereas in 1937 it made only £8.8 per car. So, who is kidding who?

Here, in much simplified form, is a summary of MG's financial performance in the 1930s:

Year Ending	Total Sales	Gross Profit	Nett Profit (Loss)
31 Dec. 1930	£394,722	£ 79,804	£ 17,763
31 Dec. 1931	£289,844	£ 50,750	(£13,046)
31 Dec. 1932	£452,960	£ 99,970	£ 24,914
31 Dec. 1933	£446,339	£ 87,789	(£ 5,186)
31 Dec. 1934	£452,448	£102,984	£ 20,859
31 Aug. 1935*	£175,571	£ 27,967	(£28,156)
31 Aug. 1936	£391,150	£ 70,899	(£16,440)
31 Dec. 1936**	£225,293	£ 43,953	£ 16,033
31 Dec. 1937	£695,590	£135,851	£ 25,436
31 Dec. 1938	£613,305	£111,547	£ 5,688
31 Dec. 1939	£424,450	£ 95,522	£ 3,727

*   This was an 8-month accounting period
**   This was a 4-month accounting period

The first case was to allow MG's accounts to be re-aligned with those of the parent company, the second case was because Morris was altering its entire corporate accounting structure. (The difference between 'gross' and 'nett' profit includes charges for company overheads.)

Further analysis of profit performance shows that:

i)   MG lost money in 1931 as sales fell away, but this was a 'slump' year for the entire British motor industry, so that can surely be excused.
ii) MG lost money in 1933 because of an exceptionally high charge for 'overhead' expense. Gross profit was still very healthy indeed.
iii) MG lost money in 1935, this being the classic case of a new management 'dumping' every possible loss into the old accounts. It happened then – it still happens today...
iv) MG lost money in 1936, a year in which the entire product range was renewed. As in 1933, gross profits were healthy, but the 'overhead' charge, caused by retooling, was high.

All in all, I am not convinced that profitability was improved when MG was swept up into Morris Motors control, and I think that this table vindicates Cecil Kimber as a good businessman who was badly served by his superiors.

the bottom of all this, and his strategy of pushing the MG business into Morris Motors ownership explained most moves.

Not only was he intent on having commercial control of MG at Cowley, he was also determined to subsume all future MG design work into the Cowley design offices at the same time. In fact, financially it made a lot of sense to insist that the design team based their new car on the latest-generation Morris/Wolseley running gear: big cost-savings were there to be made. (At about this time, incidentally, Wolseley, based in Birmingham, might also have suffered the same fate. However, under Miles Thomas, Wolseley was a little more fortunate because the business was geographically so remote from Cowley, and was a more profitable operation. Even so, from 1935 onwards, all new Wolseleys would also begin to use Morris chassis, bodies and engines, and were really no more than up-market, higher-priced versions of Morris types.)

As managing director of Morris Motors, Len Lord, you might have thought, would not have had time to concern himself with design matters; but Robert Boyle, who was nominally in charge of all mechanical design at Cowley, soon discovered otherwise! There, and for many years to come at Longbridge (when he was BMC's chairman in the 1950s), Lord was a compulsive and inventive designer. Hours would be spent around drawing boards or in styling studios, the cigarette ever-present, the hat often still on the back of his head, and the hair-trigger temper and foul-mouthed language always ready to erupt. Even so, this ambitious man, this easy-to-hate tycoon with a multitude of rough edges, was an amazingly successful businessman who knew what would sell, and somehow knew what was a practical installation. You did not have to like him – and, make no mistake, not many people did like him – to

realize this, and it had to be admitted that he had a remarkable track record.

Len Lord's inspiration – and, incidentally, that of William Rootes of the Hillman-Humber-Sunbeam-Talbot combine, too – was General Motors of Detroit. By the mid-1930s GM had already brought 'product planning' to a fine art, one which involved making innumerable different models carrying different badges, around a very limited stock of engines, body styles and structural layouts. If GM could do it, Lord concluded, so could the Nuffield Organization.

MG DESIGN STRATEGY – ALL CHANGE

When Len Lord closed down the Abingdon design office, the staff were told that they would be moved to Cowley, virtually without notice, and that they would then be integrated into the larger operation. The alternative was that they would be sacked.

Abingdon to Cowley was only a few miles – maybe fifteen minutes away, by road – but for designers like H.N. Charles and the young Jack Daniels, it was an almost complete change of culture. Although Cecil Kimber had managed to win the concession of keeping a tiny 'liaison' between the two factories in 1935, along with a small development department at Abingdon, the designers were soon bound to lose touch. Worse, they were expected to work on whatever new projects Robert Boyle directed them towards, which meant that in theory they might be involved in Morris, Wolseley or MG new models in the future. However, although this sounded depressing, it was not all bad news, for Len Lord also made it clear that he wanted to see the immediate development of not one, but a whole family of new MG models.

Len Lord (later Sir Leonard Lord, 1896 – 1967)

If Len Lord had not set up the Nuffield Organization in 1935, MG might not have been absorbed. And if he had not wanted to centralize everything at Cowley, the 'Abingdon Touch' might not have been dispersed. His contacts with MG began in the 1920s, and finally ended in 1966.

A great deal has been written about Leonard Lord, sometimes critical but mostly complimentary. Born in Coventry in 1896, he was originally apprenticed to Courtaulds (the textile company); he then joined Hotchkiss & Cie (the Coventry-based engine manufacturer), before that company was taken over by William Morris and renamed Morris Engines. From 1921 Lord's rise to prominence was swift, and he soon gained a reputation as a formidable production engineer at Morris Engines, with a very sharp and at times coarse tongue. This was where he first made contact with MG, and so with Cecil Kimber, because the original MGs got their engines from Coventry.

In 1927 William Morris sent Lord to Wolseley Motors to modernize the business, and in the early 1930s he was drafted into Cowley to do the same job on Morris Motors, as managing director. This was when he totally rationalized Lord Nuffield's ramshackle business empire – though with little thanks. Along the way he made sure that MG was swept into the new parent company, and that Abingdon's independence was destroyed; furthermore, by becoming managing director of MG at this time, he effectively demoted Cecil Kimber to general manager. Three years on, in 1936, the rationalization job was done, but after a bitter argument with Lord Nuffield about profit-sharing, Lord stormed out of the business. For the time being his links with MG were severed.

Early in 1938 he joined Austin as works director, but from the day he arrived Lord Austin let him run the design and development departments. After Lord Austin died, Len Lord became joint managing director, in 1942; and then in 1945 he became chairman and managing director. From that time until he moved into partial retirement he was the driving force, the dynamo, behind everything which Austin – and later BMC – did.

In 1948 he approached Lord Nuffield suggesting a merger, but was rebuffed, as he was when he made a further attempt in 1950; but he finally got his way in the winter of 1951/1952. The merger represented the founding of BMC, and when the ageing Lord Nuffield retired at the end of that year, Len Lord became its outright boss. From that moment on, MG was only a constituent of the British Motor Corporation. One of Len Lord's first decisions directly affected MG: he refused permission for the EX175 project to be put into production, giving precedence to the new Austin-Healey marque (this move ensured that MG developed the TF as an interim car instead).

Lord was knighted in 1954, becoming Sir Leonard. In 1956 he chose to go into partial retirement, and George Harriman became joint managing director. Before he stepped down he finally gave approval for the MGA to take over from the TF, a process which was completed in 1955. He retired from executive duties when he reached sixty-five years of age, becoming BMC's vice president; he received a peerage, and became Lord Lambury for the last years of his life.

Throughout his life he was always known as 'Len' Lord (behind his back, if not to his face), and was commonly accepted as being a real rough diamond, an organizing genius, and a vibrant, combative personality who usually chose to call a spade a 'bloody shovel'.

He finally cut his links with BMC in 1966, and died a year later.

Old men forget, and there are certain differences of opinion about what happened next, but it seems that for a time at Cowley there was a 'section leader for MG' called Jack Grimes; that a young Alec Issigonis began to exert more and more influence on suspension designs; and that H.N. Charles, Jack Daniels and George Cooper spent most of their time on MG work. Not only did this involve finishing off, and improving, the layout of the Wolseley-based SA '2-litre' model (which eventually went on sale

H. N. Charles: T-Series Top Designer

Hubert Charles was already an experienced engineer before he joined MG: he worked in the Royal Flying Corps, then in the Zenith carburettor concern, and later with Automotive Products in Leamington, before he started his Morris Motors career at Cowley in 1924. In the mid-1920s he had met and befriended Cecil Kimber, unofficially helping him with many aspects of the design of the early cars. From 1930 Charles became Kimber's chief design and development engineer, a post he held until 1935; this was when Len Lord abruptly closed down the design offices at Abingdon, moving Charles to Cowley, and putting him to work on the next generation of 'Nuffield MGs'.

Before the outbreak of World War II, Charles joined Rotol (who built aircraft propellers), and lost touch with MG. After Rotol he moved to the Austin Motor Co. at Longbridge, but he never found the chance to renew his contacts because in 1946 he left to set up his own consultancy.

with a 2.3-litre engine!), and starting project work on a new VA '1 1/2-litre' – but it also involved designing a completely new Midget, the T-Series. By all accounts, no T-Series work of any nature had been carried out at Abingdon before the abrupt change of policy direction, for Charles's team had been otherwise engaged with the R-Type and its developments, and on the still-born EX150 project. Therefore it doesn't matter how you measure it or judge it: the T-Series pedigree was born at Cowley, even though it was experienced MG men such as H.N.Charles and Jack Daniels who designed the car.

Because Len Lord had already pronounced a death sentence on the P-Type Midget and the N-Type Magnette range, almost by default the new-generation Midget, the T-Series, was going to have to take over from both of them. The style might look similar (which was good for continuity), and there would be dimensional familiarities between them. In true 'product-planning' tradition, therefore, the new T-Series ended up rather larger than the PB, and rather smaller than the N-Series Magnette. Here is a tabular comparison:

	PB Midget	T-Series Midget	N-Type Magnette
Engine	939cc	1,292cc	1,271cc
	4-cyl	4-cyl	6-cyl
	43bhp	50bhp	57bhp
Wheelbase (inches/mm)	87.3(2,217)	94(2,387)	96(2,438)
Track (inches/mm)	42(1,067)	45(1,143)	45(1,143)
Length (inches/mm)	131(3,327)	139.75(3,550)	148(3,759)
Width (inches/mm)	52.5(1,334)	56(1,422)	54(1,372)
Unladen weight (lb/kg)	1,652(758)	1,765(801)	1,960(889)
Power/weight ratio (bhp/ton) **	58.3	63.5	65.1

** This was not a figure generally quoted in the mid-1930s, so I have calculated it today. It gives a good idea of the cars' performance potential.

The only significant T-Series statistic not to fall neatly between the two older types was its body width, because at the design stage the T-Series was allowed to 'grow' a little to provide more elbow room across the rather cramped driving compartment. Compared with the PB, for instance, the cockpit was 3in (7.6cm) wider, and the car was also 4in (10cm) taller when the hood was erect.

Although it was to use a majority of modified Morris/Wolseley components which were completely different from the older types, the basic layout of the new Midget was to be very much like those earlier MG models, so the Cowley design office was able to settle the chassis and body design relatively quickly. The chassis, complete with a 94in (2,387mm) wheelbase, was brand new, though it followed every existing MG principle, being ladder style, complete with channel-section side members, and with those members passing under the line of the rear axle. The channel was boxed in alongside the engine and gearbox, and cross-bracing was by means of four tubular members, two of them linking the front of the leaf springs, one of them the rear of the rear springs.

Two six-volt batteries provided electricity, these being mounted in cradles at each side of the propeller shaft, just ahead of the line of the back axle.

By 1990s expectations (not a fair comparison, I know, but worth considering) the frame was extremely flexible in torsion, and not much better in bending; but it was nevertheless adequately stiff by the standards of the day.

Front and rear suspension were both by short, stiff, half-elliptic leaf springs – the front springs being under the line of the side-members, the rear springs being several inches outboard – pivoting on Silentbloc bearings at their front ends, and sliding through trunnions (which needed frequent greasing) at the rear. The front axle was a steel forging, the rear axle a spiral bevel design. Shock absorbing, front and rear, was by Luvax hydraulic lever arm dampers (previous MG models had usually used friction-type dampers). Steering, right-hand drive only, was by cam gear.

Although the Lockheed drum brakes were only of 9in (22.8cm) diameter – I use the word 'only' because the PA/PB and Magnette types had both used massive 12in (30.5cm) drums – they had wider shoes and were at least hydraulically operated. As ever, the handbrake lever was mounted vertically, on the left side of the floor adjacent to the gear lever, and was of the 'fly-off' type; and as one enthusiast once told me: 'When you had a girl-friend in the passenger seat it was amazing how often you had to check that that lever was still in the right place...'

Cecil Kimber was known to distrust hydraulic brakes – every previous 'Kimber' MG had been fitted with a cable-operated system – but this was one more instance where his stubbornness had let MG slip behind the times. Well proven by this time, hydraulic brakes would be used on the SA, now on the T-Series, and would then be applied to every future MG model.

Unlike the P-Type Midgets and the N-Type Magnettes, the T-Series was only meant to be sold as a two-seater open roadster, which meant that there were to be no packaging compromises – in particular no need to squeeze extra seats above and behind the front seats. The style was therefore easy to settle, for as there had never been any complaints about the rakish good looks of either the 1934-model J2, nor the PA/PB Midgets, the shape of the new T-Series car almost arranged itself. Looking very much like the PB, but subtly larger, longer and (as already mentioned) wider, the new T-Series shape was an instant classic, recognizable then and even more so today. As would become normal with all other mainstream Abingdon types, the main centre section of the shell – the tub, we would call it today – would be assembled and painted by Morris Bodies in Coventry.

Look at the PB, then look at the T-Series, and you will see the same car, just a little larger, complete with typically MG features such as the cutaway doors, the bench seat back, the wiper motor on the screen rail, the large slab fuel tank (15 imperial gallons/68 litres on this model), the exposed steering wheel, the free-standing headlamps and the total lack of bumpers. Here, if in no other feature, Cecil Kimber's influence was still strong.

MG, being confident of their own image, knew that there was no need to plaster the new car with badges. As ever, the only exterior reference to the MG marque was that famous radiator grille style (now slatted, rather than honeycomb, in detail) which

incorporated the octagon badge. At the rear, nothing at all, but then – who needed it?

NEW ENGINE AND TRANSMISSION

Compared with the previous 'Abingdon-generation' Midgets, the truly major change for the T-Series Midget was in the choice of engine and transmission: instead of using much modified and highly developed overhead-camshaft engines, it used an overhead-valve 1,292cc engine, and instead of the compact Wolseley-derived gearbox (which had no synchromesh) there was to be a different assembly which would gain synchromesh in the coming months.

In fact Len Lord told the Cowley design office to use an existing Nuffield unit, though he did authorize a considerable tune-up, and having looked around the range, the team chose the latest overhead-valve 1,292cc engine (as earmarked for the new Wolseley 10/40 and 12/48 saloons) for

Morris Bodies Branch

Right from the start, in 1913, Morris cars were assembled at Cowley, near Oxford, but always used bodyshells produced on other sites. Hollick & Pratt of Coventry was an original supplier, but Morris bought it out in 1922, renaming it the Morris Bodies Branch. Situated close to the Armstrong-Siddeley complex in Coventry, and overhanging the main Coventry-London railway line, this factory continued to supply bodyshells – not only to Morris, but later to MG and to Riley – until the end of the 1960s. Except for the Tickford-bodied TA and TB types (whose shells were erected at the Tickford factory in Newport Pagnell, Bucks, which is now the home of Aston Martin), every wooden-framed T-Series body shell was produced at the Morris Bodies Branch in Coventry.

Looking back into the archive, it is fascinating to see that T-Series shells were built in Coventry alongside shells as different as those for the RM-Series Riley, and the estate-car rear end of the Morris Minor Traveller! All were produced using the same technology, whereby the wooden framing – whether obvious or hidden away – was structural, the steel panelling then being nailed to those wooden members. In later years MGA shells would also be built in the same factory, as would the original MGBs. The MG sequence was finally destroyed in the 1970s when Pressed Steel took over complete responsibility for the MGB.

The TA Engine: a Long Nuffield Heritage

Although the TA's engine proved to be very tuneable, it was by no means a cutting-edge design in 1936. Way back in 1919, Morris Motors had started using a side-valve, three-bearing engine of 1,495cc, which featured the 'trade-mark' cylinder stroke of 102mm. In the next fifteen years or so that basic, hard-working engine was painstakingly developed as a four-cylinder, and later with a six-cylinder derivative – but always as a side-valve design.

The very first overhead-valve conversions of the four-cylinder unit – the 1,292cc and 1,548cc versions inspired by Leonard Lord at Cowley – were not completed until the mid-1930s, and were originally intended only for use in the Series II Wolseleys of 1935 and 1936. However, as soon as Len Lord persuaded Lord Nuffield to sell the MG Car Co. to Morris Motors Ltd, itself a part of the new Nuffield Organization 'holding company', he also instructed the Cowley design office to use a modified version of these engines in the new TA and, later, in the VA.

Between 1919 and 1939, this one engine family, always with the cylinder stroke of 102mm, was built in the following sizes:

Engine	Capacity (cc)
4-cylinder, side-valve:	1,292 1,548 1,802
4-cylinder, overhead-valve:	1,292 1,548 1,802
6-cylinder, side-valve:	1,818 1,938 2,062 2,288 2,561
6-cylinder, overhead-valve:	1,818 2,062 2,288 2,322 2,561

The last car usage of all was in the Wolseley 12/48, 14/60 and 18/85 saloons of the 1948 model year. The 1,802cc 'four' was used in Morris Oxford taxis as late as 1955.

---

further development. This one was actually larger, if not more powerful, than the six-cylinder engine which had been used in many Magnas and Magnettes in the 1930s. As *The Autocar* so delicately put it in 1936: 'This is in keeping with the modern trend of design, in which four-cylinder engines are regaining popularity even where engine size is increased.' As described in the panel above, it was really a final development of a Morris Engines unit which had been progressively developed since 1919. Unfortunately, although it looked suitable – in twin-SU carburettor guise it would produce 50bhp for the TA – it was always afflicted by an inefficient cylinder head, and a crankshaft which lacked counterbalance.

To make sure this rather bulky engine could be fitted into a relatively slim engine bay, the cylindrical air cleaner was mounted at the back (rather than at the side) of the aluminium inlet passage, tucked in very close to the driver's side of the bulkhead. The water temperature was regulated by a thermostat, this being another 'first' for Midgets, which had previously survived with thermo-syphon action into a high radiator top tank. As far as Len Lord was concerned, however, it was there, it was available, and it was a lot cheaper to produce than the overhead-cam units had ever been – and in any case, that was what he wanted. A 1,548cc version of the same engine was already reserved for use in the forthcoming VA, and six-cylinder derivatives were to be used in the SA and the WA which would appear in 1938.

Interestingly enough, and in spite of its mundane pedigree and technical shortcomings, this was no 'second-best' engine: the 'works' trials cars were considerably tuned, and with success, because these engines accepted supercharging without too many qualms. It was also a much simpler engine to maintain than the overhead-cam units had ever been. There was one feature which the trials specialists did not like, however, and that was the specified aluminium alloy sump pan: although it looked good, it was vulnerable to damage on the rough tracks used in reliability trials, whereas a pressed steel sump pan was more likely to bend, rather than crack open as a result of being hit by rocks; this explains why this change was often made.

In many ways, getting the engine accepted by MG customers was more of an 'image' problem than a technical one, the previous overhead-cam engines having become so specialized and so unique to MG that some die-hards were not ready to accept anything different. Even so, although they never liked to admit this at first, in every factor except its weight, this was a thoroughly suitable sports car unit. Many years ago, in *MG by McComb*, Wilson McComb made this telling comment:

> ...many MG owners found their [overhead-cam engined] cars disappointing in use, mainly because proper maintenance of the ohc engine demanded a level of mechanical skill far above that of the average *garagiste*. Correctly assembled, it was a beautiful little unit, but there has seldom been an engine that the incompetent could more readily transform into a clattering, oil-slinging abortion, barely capable of pulling the car along ... the general 'fussiness' of

the ohc models made them tiring on long journeys.

Was this all true? If so, it explains why Len Lord insisted that a more conventional Nuffield unit should be used in the new T-Series car. It was Lord, after all, who had been at Wolseley Motors at the time, who had inspired the birth of the new Wolseley-built side-valve Morris Minor unit in 1931, as a more reliable successor to the little overhead-cam engine.

To match the TA's 50bhp/1,292cc engine (Type MPJG) the designers were also obliged to use existing Nuffield clutch, gearbox and back axle designs, thus ensuring that there was absolutely no running gear 'carried over' from the PA/PB or Magnette types. The clutch was a 'corporate' Morris Motors design with a cork-faced pressure plate running in oil, and did not look promising at first, but it proved adequate for its purpose. Even so, it never had the same 'bite' as earlier (or, indeed, later) T-Series clutches.

Although the existing Nuffield four-speed gearbox which mated with the engine was not a sporting unit – and in mid-1935 it still did not have synchromesh – the designers made many improvements before the T-Series was ready to go on sale. First of all, a close-ratio set of gears was designed, a remote-control gear shift (looking similar, but actually being different from, the PA/PB/Magnette change) was added to the top of the existing cast-iron casing, and synchromesh was rushed through, to be added to top and third gears soon after the car went on sale in 1936.

Finally, a Nuffield banjo-type spiral bevel back axle, with 4.875:1 final drive ratio, was fitted. Incidentally, although this was another corporate 'building-block', it had a different track and sometimes a different ratio in other applications. This, for instance, is how the TA's axle compared with contemporary Morris and Wolseley models which also used it in 1936/1937:

	MG TA	Wolseley 10/40 and 12/48	Morris 10-4 and 12-4
Track (inches/mm)	45(1,143)	50(1,270)	50(1,270)
Final drive ratio	4.875:1	5.22:1	4.875:1

Since the new T-Series sports car's engines, gearboxes and back axles were all to be manufactured in the same Coventry factory which made other versions of the same units for Morris and Wolseley cars, economically this made good sense, for little new tooling was needed, all the manufacturing 'wrinkles' were known, and preparations could go ahead very quickly indeed. In fact work on the new car went ahead so smoothly that it was ready for announcement in June 1936. Although legend has it that new British cars could be designed quickly and easily in the 1930s, please don't believe all this sort of propaganda. Hubert Charles and his small team had been absorbed into Cowley in July 1935, and must have found the transformation upsetting; yet they managed to get an all-new – repeat, all-new – sports car ready for the market in a mere eleven months.

For MG's suppliers it was a huge achievement, too: pressings had to be sourced for the chassis frame, and the Morris Bodies branch had to prepare new press tools for the bodyshell panels, to organize the production of yet another ash-framed centre section (they were used to this – MG had always kept them busy!), and the jigging to screw it all together. Other suppliers – Lockheed for brakes, Dunlop for tyres, British Jaeger for instruments, for instance – all had to move mountains.

For Abingdon and its planners, this was just one of several changes and developments which were brewing. At the end of 1935, for instance, the workforce had been building PB sports cars and the N-Type Magnettes, and they were already preparing to build the new SA '2-litre' models. The first of the SAs would go down the raised assembly lines in April 1936, and the very first TAs were to be assembled at the end of June.

Nor was that the moment to relax, for the VA would be previewed before the end of the year, although it would be mid-1937 before any production cars were ready to be delivered.

TA ON THE MARKET

After a rather breathless year in which MG's future had been settled and – in fairness – while the public wondered what exactly was going on, the new T-Series sports car was finally unveiled. Nowadays, of course, we know it was the TA, but this only became a title retrospectively applied. The date – and mark this carefully – was 19 June 1936. Here was a new Midget full of 'firsts' : the largest yet, the first push-rod engined Midget, the first to have an engine larger than one litre, and the first to use hydraulic brakes. It was a new model for which Nuffield publicists claimed 'twenty-seven special features', though I have never actually seen those features listed. Cecil Kimber might have mistrusted what he was given to sell – for, make no mistake, he had had little influence on its design, only on its shape – but he must surely have seen the manufacturing logic of it all.

Len Lord's masterstroke was to put it on

When the TA appeared in 1936, it was the first-ever MG to use a derivative of a long-lived Morris / Wolseley four-cylinder engine family. The overhead-valve version of this engine appeared in 1937 to power the Morris 10 and Morris 12, complete with a single SU carburettor, a rather inefficient-looking exhaust manifold, and a direct-acting gearchange lever...

...while the dynamo, spark plugs and distributor were all on the left side of the engine. It was a rather lofty, long-stroke engine which had never before been used in a sports car.

the British market for £222: this was exactly the same price as the last of the PBs, but for a Midget which was larger, faster, yet probably cheaper to maintain. For the British buyer, the only bad news was that the TA was rated as a 'Ten' instead of a 'Nine', which meant that it would cost more to licence every year – 15s (75p) a year, to be exact, which was bearable. *The Autocar's* analysis of the new TA showed CJO 617, which was certainly a prototype as series production did not actually begin until chassis number TA253 was pushed down the tracks on 25 June. Sticklers for detail will want to know that there were visual differences between CJO 617 (which had trafficator indicators built into the sides of the scuttle) and the production cars. Headlined 'The Midget Grows Up', the feature ended with the summary: 'Generally speaking, the new, larger Midget should have much improved facili-

ties as a touring machine, but should have lost none of its sporting characteristics, whilst a good performance is certain to be provided.'

In those stiff-upper-lip days of motoring journalism, this was as close as any writer would go to confirming that the PB had been overdue for change, yet it was clear that the testers couldn't wait to get their hands on a production car.

The Motor, whose description followed a few days later, was rather ambiguously restrained, describing the new car merely as 'A Larger MG Midget', and sub-heading this: 'New four-cylinder model with bigger engine and longer wheelbase designed expressly for sports enthusiasts and competition work'. Len Lord would no doubt have been amused by that, for the TA was most definitely not intended for competition work, of which he disapproved. If it was designed for anything, it was to make

Another derivative of the engine that would be used in the TA was this Wolseley 12/48 type, where the SU carburettor was vertically (instead of horizontally) positioned.

As redeveloped and tuned for use in the TA, the Wolseley-type engine had twin horizontal SU carburettors, a more efficient cast exhaust manifold (which incorporated the all-important MG octagon badge), and an air-cleaner which, because it was such a tight fit under the narrow bonnet of the TA, had to be mounted behind the line of the carburettors themselves.

more money for Nuffield than any previous MG! Since road tests of MG sports cars had rather dried up since the J2 debacle of 1932 (Kimber had supplied a tuned car to *The Autocar*, customers had tried to emulate those figures without success, and several two-bearing crankshafts had been broken in the process!), a full report on the TA was awaited with great interest.

The Autocar tested JB 9447 on 18 September 1936 (by which time the synchromesh gearbox had been added), recording a two-way top speed of 77.59mph (124.84kmph) at Brooklands, along with 0–60mph (0–96.5kmph) in 23.1sec, and overall fuel consumption of 27–29mpg (10.5–9.75 litres/100km). Chief tester H.S. Linfield was photographed in the car, wrote the test himself, and commented that:

Though there are many changes noticeable in the latest Series T MG Midget ... in character the car remains of the same type. That is, it gives an unusually good performance for its engine size, handles in a distinctly better manner than the ordinary touring vehicle, and possesses those touches in the *tout-ensemble* that endear it to the owner with sporting tendencies...

On the road, the 'feel' of the car has undergone a change: the new Midget is softer, quieter, and more flexible at low speeds from the ordinary touring car angle. No car, even a sports machine, is driven fast all the time, and to be able to potter really satisfactorily is a quality worth having ... It was odd to be without the familiar exhaust burble, for there was no real sound from the tail pipe ... however, it is understood that slightly more of an 'MG note' is to be restored...

It is still a car which seems to revel in being held at a speed between 50 and 60mph [80 and 97km/h], and which, given any chance, will run up easily to a good deal more when wanted.

The TA's engine laid bare,
showing the deep cylinder
block, and the large access
hole to the camshaft
chamber and pushrods.
Note the very small
(63.5mm) cylinder bores
used in the 1,292cc
engines. Recast cylinder
blocks allowed much
wider bores (and larger
capacity engines) to be
used, as they were on MG
competition cars later in
the 1930s.

This was the bottom end
of the TA's MPJG engine,
showing that although it
had a robust crankshaft,
there were no counter-
balance weights.

The 1,292cc MPJG engine, as used in the TA, had simple combustion chambers, and was not originally intended to be super-tuned, but could produce surprisingly high power outputs for use in trials. Like post-war BMC engines, it featured siamezed inlet ports, and the exhaust ports of cylinders Nos. 2 and 3 were also siamezed.

Nothing sporting here! The TA's clutch was cork-lined and ran in a bath of oil, like all other versions of this engine and its related gearbox. Later-model T-Series cars would be rid of this obsolete type of clutch mechanism.

There was much more of the same, telling us in patriotic fashion that MG had done it again, and encouraging everyone to dash out and order a new TA. The new hydraulic brakes and the synchromesh gearbox came in for particular praise, as did the seating and driving position. One minor criticism, however, was aimed at the gimmicky '20mph [32km/h] light' which came on whenever the car was running at speeds below that limit, presumably to tell the driver he was being a good boy in the new-fangled restricted areas (introduced in 1935):

'This an excellent idea, but for night work this lamp is a little overpowering. It is understood that the necessary modification has already been incorporated.'

Linfield, a trials driver of note and a tester known to undertake regularly the long journey to and from his beloved West Country, preferably at night to avoid the dreary traffic, ended by writing: 'A "different" Midget admittedly, but one with some distinctly practical features embodied, and giving plenty of performance in an interesting way.'

Even though it was designed in the Morris Motors offices at Cowley, the TA's chassis frame was very similar to those previously evolved at Abingdon for cars like the PA Midget and the N-Series Magnette. The wheelbase was 7ft 10in (2,388mm) and the wheeltracks 3ft 9in (1,143mm), making this new frame almost Magnette-sized. Very little production tooling was needed to prepare the frame members (assembly from pieces was at Abingdon). Note the cradles for the two six-volt batteries, which were placed ahead of the line of the rear axle, also the brace member between the rear dampers behind the line of the same axle, and the neat way in which the carburettor air cleaner and trunking was kept as slim as possible. With only minor alterations, this frame would be used up until the end of TC assembly at the end of 1949.

This was the TA's rolling chassis, almost ready to have its body fixed into place. So there is some shape in those side members after all! These days, the use of a rigid steering column, pointing straight at the driver's chest, would not meet any crash-test regulations, but in the 1930s neither designers nor drivers even thought about such things.

The Light Car & Cycle Car, long-time fans of the MG marque, also tested a car at this time, noting the splendid two-way top speed of 80.36mph (129.3km/h) – 'two up', as they proudly reminded every reader – along with a standing-start quarter-mile time of 21.6sec which, if accurate, was equal to that ever achieved by any later T-Series car except the TF1500.

The TA got off to a good start in the market place, for during the summer of 1936 the first deliveries were concentrated on UK dealerships. The first twenty cars were assembled in June, more than one hundred were built in July and in August, and nearly 200 cars followed in September. Even at this stage, of course, change and improvements were being made to the production car, for a part-synchromesh gearbox was added from engine MPJG 684, while the promised modifications were made to the exhaust note (Cecil Kimber agreed to these

merely by listening to cars as they drove past him!). Len Lord, on the other hand, was not around to see if his idea of an MG Midget was successful, for he had left the Nuffield Organization on 27 August 1936, vowing never-ending enmity to Lord Nuffield and all his works!

No doubt to the surprise of the MG diehards, the TA was a success. PAs and PBs had sold steadily, but rarely at more than 100 cars a month, and as MG knew but would not always admit, warranty and repair costs had been relatively high. Even before their reputation became widely known, the TA began to sell at the typical rate of 150 cars a month. The point was not only that the TA cost no more than its predecessor, but that it was a larger, more comfortable, and more restful car to drive, too – in effect, it was an N-Type Magnette (£280) at a PB price, and MG salesmen made much of that.

The TA and its British Rivals

When the TA was launched in June 1936, MG was already the dominant British maker of lower-price sports cars. It was, in fact, a very restricted class, effectively with only five models in it. These were:

BSA Scout (1,203cc)	£159.50
MG TA Midget (1,292cc)	**£222.00****
Morgan 4/4 (1,122cc)	£194.25
Singer Le Mans (972cc)	£215.00
Triumph Southern Cross (1,232cc)	£278.00

** The TA Tickford, complete with drop-head coupe bodywork, was not introduced until August 1938, at a price of £269.50.

Of the five, only the Morgan and Singer types were serious competitors. The BSA Scout, even though it had front-wheel drive and was therefore technically interesting, had no sporting pedigree, while the Triumph Southern Cross was too heavy and too old-fashioned (and would be dropped within months). Except for its rock-hard suspension, the Morgan was a fine car, but it was built in very small numbers (no more than five cars a week at first). The Singer was a useful sports car with a high-revving overhead-cam engine, but it was not quite as successful as the MG.

In the end it was MG's motor-sporting reputation, and a well established dealer network (cars were mainly sold through Morris dealerships) which gave it such an advantage.

The new TA, as unveiled in 1936, looked remarkably like the last of the PBs, and had the same basic proportions. Sold only as a two-seater, it was the epitome of mid-1930s MG style, which would live until to the end of the 1940s.

This was the frontal aspect of the TA, which would soon become famous all over the world. Those were the days when the radiator was real, when there were no front bumpers, and when all lights – headlamps, driving lamp and sidelamps – stuck bravely out into the breeze. 19in wheels were normal in those days, though we would think them ludicrously over-sized today. Note the folded-down screen in this pose, as used by many drivers when the weather was right. The number plate was meaningless, except to indicate that this was the new MG T-Series, UK price £222.

The TA was a simple car to build, and also to service, because it could be taken apart like a Meccano set. The spare wheel bolted to the fuel tank, the fuel tank bolted to the rear of the bodyshell, the doors could easily be separated from their hinges, and the hood was no more than a five-minute assembly job! The owners loved it that way.

Once again to quote *MG by McComb*, MG racing expert Reg Jackson had this to say after delivering a car to an MG dealer in Manchester: 'For the first half of the journey I thought I'd never get used to it, but when I arrived I said to myself, "Jackson, you've never felt less tired". There wasn't much wrong with the T-Type, and it was a bloody lovely ride after getting your guts thumped out in the earlier cars.'

All this, mind you, was with a sports car available in one form, and one form only: the two-door open roadster, for MG had originally decided not to offer any four-seater or special-bodied versions of the same chassis design.

AIRLINE COUPE – AN ODDITY

Just before Christmas in 1937 – eighteen months after the TA had originally been launched – MG introduced (or should we say, 'approved of'?) a new derivative: the only closed version of the TA ever put on sale, calling it the 'Airline Coupe'. However, even by 1930s standards it was a half-hearted project, for the announcement made no headlines at all: *The Motor* mentioned it once in a rather throwaway illustrated paragraph, while *The Autocar* and *The Light Car* ignored it completely. Then in 1938 just two customers actually bought a coupe, thus making sure that it was not a myth – it was rare, it was expensive, but it was not a myth.

The new derivative was to have a closed coupe bodyshell by Carbodies of Coventry, its style being a logical mixture of TA front end with an Airline style virtually the same as that seen on PA and PB Midgets, and NA Magnette models, from 1934. Structurally the cabin was unique, for the screen was fixed, there were new doors

43

The chrome-plated luggage rack was one of several popular TA accessories. Those were the days, incidentally, when the rear tail-lamp incorporated in the rear number-plate lamp was the only rearward-facing lens.

The TA was a narrow but well equipped two-seater, only ever built in this right-hand-drive guise, with the rev-counter in the driver's line of sight and the speedometer facing the passenger. The speedometer registered up to 105mph (169km/h) – though there was no chance of attaining it in this car, whose true top speed was about 75/80mph (120/128km/h). The handbrake was of the 'fly-off' variety.

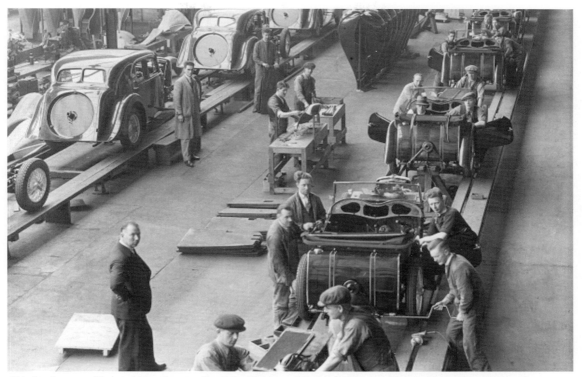

TA final assembly at Abingdon in the late 1930s, with SA '2-litre' models on the parallel track. Note the rack of TA front wings, ready for fixing at this point. The facia-panel 'station' occurs further along the track. This was a very simple assembly line, where the cars were moved forwards by a hefty push from the workforce.

hinged at the front, sliding sidescreens, and a smoothly detailed fastback coupe roof, complete with trafficators behind the door apertures.

Inside the cabin, armrests were recessed into the side of the door trims, which also had specially recessed waistlines to increase the across-shoulders dimension. The interior woodwork was in polished walnut, including the instrument panel itself, and deep pile carpets were fitted to the floor.

At the launch it was stated that the body was '...by Carbodies, produced under the supervision of H.W. Callingham, the well known specialist in bodywork design' – although Callingham's involvement was

only as the marketing agent, for his premises were in central London. To produce this car, MG in fact proposed to supply partly completed TA shells from the Morris Bodies branch in Coventry, to Carbodies, also of Coventry but about one mile away, across the city centre. Painted and trimmed shells would then be transported to Abingdon in the usual way, and Callingham was to have the rights to sell the finished product.

Since one car had already been made so that pictures for the launch could take place, I assume that only one further Airline Coupe was ever sold, which must make this a commercial failure by any measure! The problem was undoubtedly the price,

Another Abingdon assembly-shot from the period, this being at the pre-body-mount stage. The chassis in the foreground is one of the SA/VA 'touring MG' family, the TA chassis line being furthest from the camera, with completed SAs being checked out in the background.

Close relation! The VA model, announced in the autumn of 1936, was larger, heavier and not nearly as sporting as the TA, though it shared the same basic engine, gearbox and axle assemblies. The engine, however, was a 1,548cc unit, the wheelbase was 9ft (2,743mm), and every car was a four-seater, either saloon, DHC or tourer.

H. N. (Hubert) Charles was the gifted designer who interpreted all Cecil Kimber's ideas, until he left Nuffield in the late 1930s. Much of the technical credit for the TA/TB/TC Midgets should go to him.

because at £295 – which was £73, or one-third, more than the normal TA – it was obviously too expensive for most prospective buyers. Maybe £73 looks to be a trifling amount these days, but in 1937 one could certainly have bought a two-year-old 8hp saloon car for the same amount. It must have been the price, rather than the small two-seater cabin which made the Airline unsaleable, but anyway MG seemed to lose interest in it within weeks of launch. In any case, by the autumn of 1938 it had other special-body concerns, namely in the shape of the TA Tickford.

TA (1936 – 1939)

Numbers Built :
3,003 (of which 260 were Tickford DHC, and two were TA Airline Coupe)
Production period : June 1936 – April 1939

Layout
Ladder-type separate steel chassis frame, with steel panelled body panels on a wooden bodyshell skeleton. Two-door, front engine/rear drive, sold as a two-seater open sports car, or as a two-seater Tickford-bodied drop-head coupe.

Engine

Type	Nuffield, Type MPJG
Block material	Cast iron
Head material	Cast iron
Cylinders	4 in-line
Cooling	Water
Bore and stroke	63.5 x 102mm
Capacity	1,292cc
Main bearings	3
Valves	2 per cylinder, operated by in-line overhead valves, pushrods and rockers, with camshaft mounted in block, driven by chain from crankshaft
Compression ratio	6.5:1
Carburettors	2 SU
Max. power	50bhp @ 4,500rpm
Max. torque	Not quoted

Transmission
Four-speed manual gearbox. First 183 cars with no synchromesh, all other cars with synchromesh on top and third gears

Clutch	Single plate, cork facings, running in oil

Overall gearbox ratios
(Non-synchromesh)

Top	4.875
3rd	6.92
2nd	10.73
1st	18.11
Reverse	23.26
Final drive	4.875:1 (spiral bevel)

(Synchromesh on top and third, from engine no. MPJG 684)

Top	4.875
3rd	6.44
2nd	9.95
1st	16.84
Reverse	21.64
Final drive	4.875:1 (spiral bevel)

16.64mph (26.77km/h)/1,000 engine rpm in top gear

Suspension and steering

Front	Beam axle, half-elliptic leaf springs, Luvax hydraulic lever-arm dampers
Rear	Live (beam) axle, with half-elliptic leaf springs and Luvax hydraulic lever-arm dampers
Steering	Cam-gear
Tyres	4.50-19in cross-ply
Wheels	Centre-lock wire spoke
Rim width	2.5in

Brakes

Type	Drum brakes at front, drums at rear, hydraulically operated
Size	9 x 1.5in front and rear drums

Dimensions (in/mm)

Track	
Front	45/1143mm
Rear	45/1143mm
Wheelbase	94/2388mm
Overall length	139.75/3550mm
Overall width	56/1422mm
Overall height (hood erect)	53/1346mm
Unladen weight	1,765lb/800kg

UK Retail Price

2-seater Sports	£222	(£225 from May 1939)
Tickford-bodied DHC	£269.50	(£270 from May 1939)
Airline Coupe	£295	(Announced December 1937)

3   TBs and Tickfords: T-Series Rarities

Two years after the TA had first gone on sale, MG was ready to add another derivative to its range. Launched in August 1938, the Tickford-bodied drop-head coupe was a smart, short-lived, but successful version of this car – and of the TB, which followed in 1939. Because MG was not capable of building its own bodyshells at Abingdon it was, of course, quite accustomed to buying in complete bodies from outside sources. Although the Morris Bodies branch (of Coventry) was the mainstream supplier, independent coachbuilders such as

Carbodies (of Coventry), Charlesworth (of Gloucester) and Tickford (originally Salmons, from Newport Pagnell) all gained valuable contracts.

Each had its own specialities, that of Tickford being in building smart, versatile and remarkably cheap drop-head coupe styles. These were matched to a more luxuriously trimmed interior (usually with different seats, carpets and facia), and the fold-back soft-top was nicely trimmed and finished. It all added class – and weight, too. And having proved their worth with

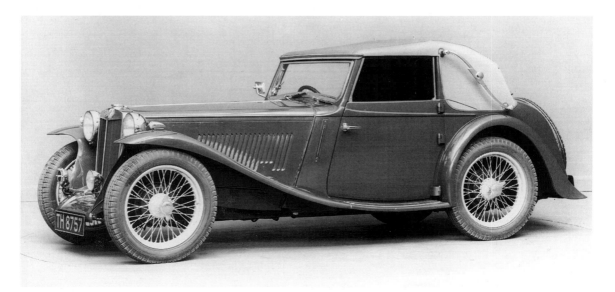

The Tickford-bodied T-Series model was only produced for a year, between the summer of 1938 and the summer of 1939. Except for the bonnet, wing and running-board panels, the Tickford shell was totally different from that of the original roadster.

The T-Series Tickford model featured a three-position hood. Here, in the 'half-erect' coupe-de-ville position, the frame has been erected, but the section above the passengers' heads has been furled back. This was the prototype, with slightly different styling.

other members of Britain's 'Big Six' – that not only could they build smart, coachbuilt shells down to a price, but they could also meet volume and delivery requirements – they were then hired to produce shells for late-1930s MG models.

The first Tickford-bodied MG to meet its public was the SA drop-head coupe; this was launched in 1936, and was soon joined by the VA drop-head coupe. Although both types were significantly more expensive than the four-door saloons, they sold well, and encouraged MG to repeat the trick in 1938, this time on the TA. This was a full-blooded attempt to expand the appeal of the T-Series, and it was a brave move. Earlier Midgets had been too small to be burdened by such a heavy body style, while an earlier, half-hearted attempt to sell the TA 'Airline' coupe had been a dismal failure, as we have seen. With the Tickford style, however, MG had a major marketing advantage, in that Tickford shells were now found on all manner of cars, occasionally even on Rolls-Royce types. Without having to stress the point, therefore, MG could sell a TA Tickford as a rather up-market version of the sports car.

Projects matured more quickly in those days, than they could possibly do so today. So although the deal was no doubt agreed early in 1938, Tickford moved from 'good idea' to 'production supply' in a mere six months. In that time they had to complete the design, lay down whatever jigging and assembly fixtures were needed, arrange to have major new individual panels (such as door skins) made in quantity, and move the first painted and trimmed shells across to Abingdon.

To get the Tickford project under way, MG sent the first TA rolling chassis (TA/2187) to Newport Pagnell in March 1938. This particular car was completed in

The TA Tickford looked good from most angles, but the fold-back hood was unavoidably more bulky that the simple build-it-yourself soft-top of Abingdon's own roadsters.

June 1938, it returned to Abingdon and Cowley for approval, and was then followed by the first batch of production shells in August 1938. The new shell incorporated semaphore direction indicators at each side of the scuttle, and there was a neat telescopic steering column; the TA open two-seater had neither of these features.

Since the TA Airline project had been such a non-event, MG must have been wary of the Tickford's reception – but they need not have worried, especially as the price was set at £269.50; this was significantly less than that of the Airline, for a much more versatile and 'classy' body style. Because it looked so smart, and because it was such a nicely equipped little two-seater, the Tickford-bodied car always received the friendliest of receptions. *The Autocar* described it as a:

> ...most attractive little two-seater, and a genuine drop-head coupe without makeshifts or compromises. It can be used as a completely closed car, when the well

padded head with its toggle irons presents a smart appearance, and the solid construction should make it draught-proof, without wind noise, and free from rattles ... the windows are of full size and operated by winding handles.

Besides the fully closed position there are two alternatives. In a few seconds the taut peak of the hood can be undone, and rolled neatly back to form a coupe de ville. Finally, the cant rails may be undone at the front end, folded back laterally, the toggle irons 'broken' and the head folded flat down to open the body completely to the sunshine and fresh air.

The gamble – and gamble it was, for there was already quite a history of slow-selling special-bodied MG sports cars – soon paid off at Abingdon. In the remainder of 1938 no fewer than 223 TA rolling chassis were allocated to Tickford – and this must have been at least half of all T-Series assembly at this period – while another thirty-seven TA Tickfords would be completed in the

---

Tickford: Bespoke Body-Builders

Although only 320 drop-head coupe bodies were built for the TA and TB models by Tickford in 1938 and 1939, the heritage of that company is long and distinguished. Tickford, in fact, was the trade name of a particular line of bodies built by Salmons & Sons at Newport Pagnell, in buildings which are now the home of Aston Martin.

Salmons & Sons was founded way back in the 1820s, when it originally built horse-drawn carriages, but bodies for cars followed as soon as the first 'horseless-carriages' took to our roads. The first 'Tickford' body of 1925 was actually a name given to a particular type of folding landaulette style, in which the soft-top could be retracted (or erected) by means of a series of cogs and a handle! By the 1930s, however, all Salmons' coachwork had come to be called 'Tickford', and the business had expanded, producing batches of standardized coachwork for Hillman, Rover and Vauxhall. The first MG business came at that time, for a four-seater drop-head coupe style on the '2-litre' SA model, then on the 1 1/2-litre VA, and finally – from August 1938 – for the TA Midget.

In the late 1930s Tickford did so much work for MG that an entire factory department was devoted to these contracts; but these were all cancelled when war broke out in 1939, and were never renewed thereafter.

---

spring of 1939. The same body style would continue when the TB was phased in during 1939, sixty of those cars having the Tickford style.

It is interesting to remember just how important T-Series assembly was to the entire Abingdon operation at this time, because from a total output of 2,500 MGs in 1938, 1,017 of them (or 40 per cent) were TAs. They were all right-hand drive, of course, which may explain why only 126 cars were exported (three of them with Tickford bodies): thirty went to Germany, twenty-four to Australia and eleven to Malaya, but fewer than ten to any other export territory. Those were the days, incidentally, when MG motoring was almost unknown in the USA, for only three TAs were shipped that way in 1938. No figures are available for 1936, unfortunately, but all in all it looks as if fewer than twenty TAs and TBs were ever exported to the USA, and a similar number to Canada.

Yet this was a period when nothing stood still at Abingdon for very long. No sooner had the TA Tickford been introduced than preparations for a new T-Series Midget – the TB, as we now know it – got under way. Visually there would be nothing to show, but there would be a new engine under the skin.

XPAG: A NEW GENERATION OF ENGINE

When Morris introduced a new generation of 10hp saloon, the Series M, in 1938, it launched a brand-new type of overhead-valve four-cylinder engine, the 39bhp 1,140cc XPJM. At a casual glance this looked like yet another design of the old unit, but it was actually completely different, and within six months a tuned-up version would be used in the next MG Midget, the TB.

For Nuffield this was a major new investment, not only in design engineering, but in facilities to build the units, for this was the very first new engine to be built in a new 35-acre Morris Engines factory at Courthouse Green, in the northern outskirts of Coventry. The first units were

Morris Engines developed an all-new-generation power unit for the Morris Ten Series M, to be launched in the autumn of 1938. It was smaller, lighter, more compact and more efficient than the older types, and would soon be tuned for use by MG.

completed there early in 1938, in a factory whose buildings already employed 4,000 people, covered 400,000 square feet and could turn out up to 4,000 engines every week. Even though it was to be badly bombed during the blitz of Coventry, this would become the Nuffield powerhouse for the next two decades – and even after the foundation of BMC in the 1950s it was still a vital part of the empire. Specialized engines (including the supercharged record car units) and the future MGA twin-cam units were all developed on this site.

Looking back, it is easy to see why the Nuffield Organization needed to introduce a new engine range for its family cars – and when it was introduced it was already long overdue; the fact that British motoring taxation still traditionally favoured small bore/long stroke power units was no excuse. As the 1930s progressed, Morris cars had relied on three families of old-fashioned side-valve engines which were at once tall, heavy and inefficient. Overhead-valve versions of each engine evolved in the mid-1930s, initially for use in Wolseleys, and it was a modified version of one of them, the MPJG, which was used in the TA. Like the BMC B-Series engines which followed in the 1950s, and which would be used in the MGA and MGB sports cars, these engines did not have very efficient heads and porting, for they were 'five-port' types, with siamezed inlet ports, and the central exhaust ports were also siamezed.

Two fascinating articles by *The Autocar*'s technical editor, Montague Tombs, published in November 1939, show just how this new engine had come to be designed. These comparisons, extracted from those articles, show why a new engine could be so useful to MG:

	New Series M (XPJM)	Old Series III (MPJM)
Head	8-port	5-port
Crankshaft	Counter-balanced	Non-counter-balanced
Capacity (cc)	1,140	1,292
Bore (mm)	63.5	63.5
Stroke (mm)	90	102
Compression ratio	6.5:1	6.0:1
Peak power (bhp)	39	37
@ RPM	@ 4,600	@ 4,500
Peak torque (lb.ft)	41	34
Weight of complete unit (including clutch and gearbox) (lb/kg)	363(165)	426(193)

In other words, the new short-stroke engine was more powerful, with more torque, able to rev more freely, and it was also 63lb/28.5kg lighter. This was exactly the result expected from a design team who had studied every aspect of their previous offerings, and improved upon them. Cutaway, or 'exploded', drawings of the new engine showed that it was, indeed, more compact than the type it replaced, with a counter-balanced crankshaft and a much shorter stroke than before. Significantly it had a very modern-looking cylinder head, with individual inlet and exhaust ports, and clearly there was also scope for the cylinder bore to be increased considerably. In addition, the new engine featured shell bearings instead of metalled bearings for the connecting-rod big ends – as my 22-year-old TA once ran a metalled bearing when I owned it in 1959, I could see why it had been done !

Monty Tombs' narrative included these jems:

When this engine was requested, a major point was that weight must be saved – a lot of weight. Something drastic had to be done... and one obvious way to do it was to shorten the stroke, for a short stroke means shorter cylinder barrels, a smaller crank chamber, and shorter throws for the crankshaft ... the cylinder barrels are entirely separate, and are surrounded by uninterrupted water spacing....

The starting point in laying out a new design is the inlet valve... It is accepted that a correctly designed engine, not supercharged, will produce its highest torque at a point in its speed range where the gas flow through the inlet valve is travelling at approximately 135ft/sec. The maximum brake horsepower is delivered when this gas flow is at approximately 240ft/second... so it is a fact that the design of the inlet valve and throat is the keynote of the engine....

Like the overhead-valve engine conversions

For use in the 1939-model Morris Ten Series M, the XPJM engine would eventually be much modified, for use in the TB and later MGs. But not with this gearchange, or that carburation!

It needed real vision to see this gentle little 39bhp/1,140cc Nuffield engine turned into a sports-car unit for the MG Midget. It was, however, 63lb (28.5kg) lighter than the older engine used in the TA, and had a much more efficient cylinder head.

developed in the mid-1930s for MG, Morris and Wolseley models, this new design had been inspired by Len Lord, for work had started in 1935/1936, just months before he stormed out of Cowley. Then, as now, it takes time to turn a 'good idea' into prototypes, and even longer to prepare production-line machinery, but the first series of engines were finally assembled in Coventry in the summer of 1938. By the time *The Autocar*'s analysis was published, the MG version of the new engine – coded XPAG – had been revealed for the MG TB sports car; but when the all-new engine appeared in October 1938, no one suspected that a version might be destined for an MG sports car. Although the XPAG later became justifiably famous, it started its life very quietly, because neither the engine nor the TB sports car which it powered got any publicity at first.

TB: SECOND THOUGHTS ARE OFTEN BETTER...

The last TA of all, carrying chassis number 3253, was built at Abingdon on 17 April 1939. Three weeks later, on 11 May, it was followed by the very first TB to be listed in Abingdon's records (chassis number 0253 – presumably 0251 and 0252 count as 'pilot-build' cars, and had been constructed earlier). This was when a telescopic steering column was standardized in the open tourer, as it had always been in the Tickford model.

British enthusiasts were not told about this new model at the time: home market deliveries began unannounced and continued throughout the summer of 1939, and some buyers, I have no doubt, did not even realize what they were getting! In fact the first time they were told about the new

Compared with the cylinder head used in TA Midgets – see page 37 –the new XPJM/XPAG layout was more compact and more efficient. This time there were individual ports for every valve and, as MG enthusiasts later discovered, much scope for super-tuning.

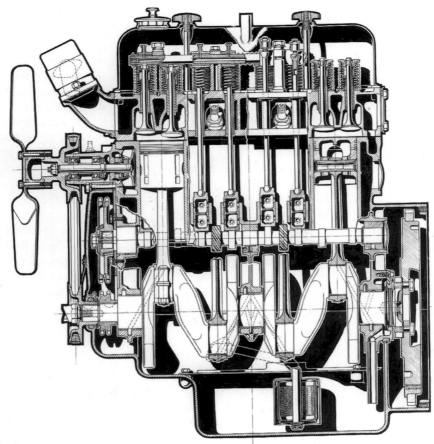

This was the cross-section of the XPAG engine for T-Series cars, as used in all models except the TA. Note the sturdy detailing of the crankshaft, including the counter-balance weights.

TB/XPAG combination was when MG production was actually being suspended at the outbreak of World War II! Although a minor increase in MG sports car prices *had* been announced in May 1939 (significantly, this was in the same week as TB series production began), no mention of the TB was made at that time. Two-seater T-Series prices went up from £222 to £225, while Tickford-bodied cars were to be priced at £270 instead of £269.50. Why was this?

Technically, and for marketing reasons, I would have expected MG to have made much of such an engine change – which was an improvement in every way. The real reason for this modesty, it seems, is that MG was actually rather ashamed of what it had just done, since compared with the TA which had been an RAC '10hp' car, the new TB was to be an RAC '11hp' car. Because annual British 'road fund' taxation was linked directly to the piston area (and therefore to the cylinder bore dimension) of a car's engine, this had long encouraged manufacturers to offer narrow bore/long stroke engines. Accordingly, when MG moved from a 63.5mm/1,292cc (TA) engine to a 66.5mm/1,250cc (TB) engine, the RAC horsepower rating went up from 10 to 11.

In 1939, when the TB slipped quietly into production, this meant an immediate rise from £7.50 to £8.25 in the annual licence fee; but as the Chancellor of the Exchequer had already announced a big increase in rating for 1940, this really meant a rise from £12.50 to £13.75. At the beginning of 1939, therefore, it cost only £7.50 to licence a TA for a year, but in 1940 it was going to cost £13.75 to licence a TB! The outbreak of war in fact made all this irrelevant, but it caused something of a furore in 1939 when it was forecast. Today, no doubt, these figures may seem meaningless, and even trivial – but sixty years later, and to allow for inflation, you should multiply by a factor of about forty, and this would mean an annual licence *increase* of £250 (late 1990s values), an impressive rise!

Although it was offering a little more power (54bhp at 5,200rpm, compared with 50bhp at 4,500rpm), this barely showed up in improved performance, nor were there any styling changes. MG was therefore asking its British customers to pay a lot more annual taxation with little improvement – so was it any wonder that there was an air of secrecy surrounding the new model? There was, however, another major improvement to the running gear, for the TB was given a newly developed version of the existing Nuffield four-speed gearbox, this one having slightly different indirect ratios, synchromesh on top, third *and* second gears, and a Borg & Beck single

Compare this XPAG engine/gearbox study with the XPJM engine shown on page 35. Apart from using twin SU carburettors and a more efficient (and MG-badged!) exhaust manifold, there was also a remote-control gearchange and a short, stubby lever.

This nearside view of the XPAG engine shows the distributor, sparking plugs and dynamo all neatly grouped together, the oil breather from the cylinder block (modern emissions regulations would outlaw that!), and the 'MG' badging on the cylinder block to confirm that this is a 1,250cc unit.

dry-plate clutch (instead of the TA variety, which had featured cork pads, running in oil). At the same time, and to match the higher-revving qualities of the XPAG engine, the rear axle ratio was changed, from 4.875:1 (TA) to 5.125:1 (TB); although this lowered the overall gearing by a barely noticeable 5 per cent, no one seemed to complain.

The styling was not changed, nor were any distinctive badges fitted, so as before, the TB was available with a choice of body styles: the Morris Bodies branch open seater, and the more luxuriously appointed Tickford drop-head coupe. There was no sign of the Airline coupe style of the TA.

All of which meant that as far as the Abingdon workforce was concerned, this was a very easy changeover, as there was no change to the general chassis or body layouts, and no change to the assembly process; neither was there any external change to the gearbox or rear axle.

Because World War II broke out on 3 September 1939, the TB had a very short run indeed. By the end of September, when the last 'pre-war' MGs had been built at Abingdon, only 379 TBs had been built, of which sixty were equipped with Tickford bodies. In retrospect, the Chancellor's forecast of an RAC tax increase had hit MG hard: in 1938 1,017 TAs had been built, but in 1939 (not a full year, admittedly) only 572 TAs and TBs were completed. On average, about twenty TAs were produced every week in 1938: a typical TB figure was fifteen.

To emphasize the discreet launch of the TB, no cars were ever supplied to the press for road tests, so we do not know what its capabilities actually were in 1939, while using pre-war quality premium fuel. I have searched, and found no figures, though *The Light Car* borrowed a TB Tickford in September 1939, commenting on all the new model's qualities, but not providing facts and figures.

WAR-TIME NOSTALGIA

Nine months after the outbreak of war, *The Autocar's* H. S. Linfield wrote lovingly about the TB which Abingdon had lent him for extended use in the spring of 1940. In spite of all the restrictions which were crowding in upon Britain's drivers, there was still time for a nostalgic look back at the pleasures of open-air motoring. The TB was delivered to him brand-new, and complete with a 'black-out' mask over one of its headlamps, and although it was obliged to run on the awful 72-octane 'pool' petrol which had been imposed, clearly it was still a real pleasure to this experienced tester:

It took the mind back several years, flicking the dust off a certain chromium-plated radiator, surmounted by an octagonal cap. I remembered doing the same thing, and checking over the oil level, topping up the radiator, and having a last look round many of its predecessors on similar occasions ... There is something about the modern MG that 'gets you', just as perhaps years ago, as in my own case, the earlier models 'got' you. An open body always helps ... But there is more than the appeal of the open car: an unroadworthy MG has never been put out, and they have always built into these cars an inherent stability, an accuracy of steering and power of stopping, which make them safe to drive fast. The familiar slogan [Safety Fast: author] has more point than most of its kind...

As this was a period when it was considered anti-social to drive fast (unless, that is, one was on urgent government business...), no performance figures were taken, and much was made of the pleasures of 50mph (80kmph) cruising but:

There was, however, a rather joyous mile or two of by-pass, a perfect surface, clear of traffic, and with a beautifully radiused right-hand bend that you can take hard over to the right-hand kerb since it is a twin-track road. For that short time and one other brief section the MG came to life for the first time in its career, which I hope will be a satisfactory one, and never allow it to be said that this was a car that was 'beaten' when it was young ! My conscience is clear.

There is no sideways 'give' when cornering fast, and the steering, though light, is nicely accurate and firm, but the springing is a great improvement for comfort over the old [pre-T-Series: author] types. You notice the difference between various kinds of surface, and feel fairly appreciable movement over the less good ones, but never real shock.

In a multi-week test, Linfield reckoned on an overall fuel consumption of 36mpg (7.9 litres/100km) – which reflected how gently one was obliged to drive in those war-torn days. Even so: 'It would be difficult to find a car of similar liveliness and all-round performance – interesting performance – that would be as economical...'

To someone so weighed down by the exigencies of conflict, clearly this had been a very special experience.

WAR: AN END TO TB ASSEMBLY

Although Britain officially declared war on

Germany on 3 September 1939, this cataclysm had looked inevitable for months; once German troops had marched into Czechoslovakia in March 1939, British politicians knew that they could no longer trust or negotiate with the German Chancellor, Adolf Hitler. Although re-armament had been building up steadily for some time, many car companies like MG had done little more than make contingency plans; when war eventually did break out, Cecil Kimber reasoned, MG private car production would have to end, and the factory would have to turn to essential work instead.

Once war had been declared, car production was speedily wound up. By the end of September, it seems, the last pre-war TBs and the last SA/VA/WA types had all been completed. Plans for 1940 models were revealed immediately after war broke out, but were never implemented (although what would become the Y-Series saloon

was mothballed). At the Morris Bodies branch in Coventry, the cheap and cheerful jigging and all the other assembly facilities for bodyshells were swept aside, and at Abingdon all the existing stock of parts was removed from the Pavlova works, soon to find storage in the St Helen's Clothing factory in Abingdon. According to the records, the very last TB of all to be built carried chassis no. TB/0610. At the time, no one could have had any idea of the length of the conflict which was to follow, but it was assumed that the TB would eventually return in its still-new guise.

MG's wartime activities are now well chronicled, these covering everything from tank repair and maintenance to producing mounting frames for aero-engines, and from building tank gun-turrets, complete nose sections for Armstrong-Whitworth Albemarle aircraft, and complete wing spars for Hawker Tempest fighters. Because it took time for sizeable military

Space, but only just, for the XPAG engine to fit under the TB (and later the TC) bonnet. The packaging problem was not height, but width, which explains why the air cleaner is mounted between the SU carburettors, and above the engine's tappet cover.

contracts to come through, Abingdon's workforce dropped alarmingly at first, but it eventually soared to 1,400, of which no fewer than 40 per cent were women. By 1945 the sheer variety of military output from buildings which had once seen sports cars being produced, was quite remarkable. It included the reconditioning of light and Matilda tanks, complete assembly of Crusader tanks, and the conversion of hundreds of tanks for special purposes (including use as armoured bulldozers and 'flail'-equipped machinery for exploding landmines).

Albemarle nose-section assembly (for delivery to Gloucester, where final assembly of the aircraft took place) was the most complex of all. In fact this twin-engined Armstrong-Whitworth medium-range bomber, which had been specifically designed to use 'non-strategic' light-alloy metals and some wood panelling, turned out to be a full blown, classic 'turkey' by almost any standards; nevertheless the RAF took delivery of 600 of them before production ended in 1944, using many for glider tugs, and as trainers for dropping parachute troops.

NO BOMBING – A CHARMED LIFE

Amazingly, in the six years of war which followed, the Abingdon factory was never bombed, although the parent company at Cowley received its share of high explosives and incendiary bombs. On the other hand, both of MG's main supply factories in Coventry – Morris Engines and Morris Bodies branch – were very badly hit. At Courthouse Green, Morris Engines was badly bombed in November 1940, and again attacked in 1941, but was back in full production within six weeks of each attack.

Morris Bodies, which was involved in making aircraft (particularly wooden) components and sections, fared much worse in the same raids, eventually being reduced to only one third of its full size, its staff dropping to a mere 600.

Structurally, therefore, there were no casualties at Abingdon, but serious damage at the supply plants. The main loss – crippling, according to many MG lovers and employees of the period – was that Cecil Kimber was forced out of office in November 1941. On the surface, Kimber's sacking was caused by MG's refusal to fall more closely into line with the remainder of Nuffield's war-time activities, but the real reason was that Kimber had come to disagree with Nuffield's vice-chairman, Miles Thomas, on almost every issue.

Thomas, a one-time journalist on *The Motor*, had joined Morris Motors in the 1920s, rising rapidly through the advertising, publicity and marketing ranks to become managing director of Wolseley Motors in 1936. Returning to Cowley as Lord Nuffield's vice-chairman in 1940, and therefore becoming Kimber's immediate superior, the two soon found ways to be at variance. You may not agree with Thomas's view of the situation in 1941, but this is what he later wrote in his autobiography, *Out on a Wing*:

> Cecil Kimber, like Nuffield, was an individualist ... He was a brave man, and took periodic wiggings for lack of profit-making with impudent *sang-froid* ... he was an originator; he designed special radiators for the cars he was sponsoring; had everything possible made octagonal – instrument cases, radiator badges, steering-wheel centre; in fact, as someone said, everything except the road wheels themselves. This kind of philosophy was all right during peacetime, but when Kimber

wanted to maintain his acute individualism after the war had broken out and adopt a policy of nonconformity when he was supposed to be working to Ministry specifications, it was clear that there had to be change.

Confirming this, John Thornley once commented that: 'Kim was sacked because of petty jealousy. Thomas was green-eyed about the extent to which Kim had the Old Man's ear ... getting the aircraft contract gave Miles Thomas the excuse to fire him.' The result was that Kimber, the founder of MG, was sacked at a moment's notice, cleared his desk and left Abingdon, never to return.

Although 'Pop' Propert stayed on as MG's general manager, he was strictly controlled from Cowley by Harold Ryder, a long-serving Nuffield manager with no interest in sports cars, but a good businessman who could keep Abingdon operating at

full stretch throughout the war.

And full stretch it certainly was. To quote Cecil Cousins, who was still one of MG's mainstays: 'What we did before the war was nothing to what we achieved during the war.'

'BITSY', A TB 'SPECIAL'

Perhaps the most famous MG oddity to come out of World War II was 'Bitsy', a versatile little tug made up by the MG workforce in the first few months of the war, for pulling loads all around the Abingdon factory, and especially for trekking to and from the St Helen's storage facility in Abingdon itself. The name 'Bitsy' for this one-off machine was immediately obvious, since it was made up of 'bits of this, and bits of that'. *The Autocar*, so short of good motoring stories to relate during the first year of the war, made much of 'Bitsy', publishing a full

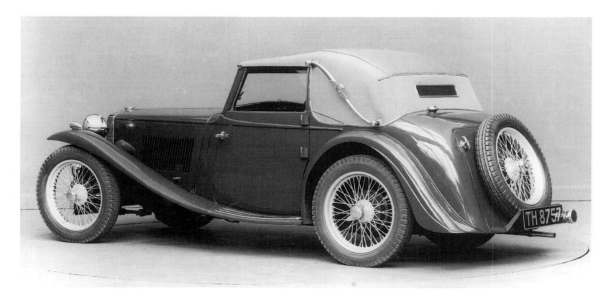

The prototype TA Tickford-bodied car featured an enclosed fuel tank in the tail, though I believe that all production Tickfords reverted to the exposed tank layout.

description in April 1940 and headlining the story: 'An MG hybrid, used for towing, which would delight a trials enthusiast'!

Based on an amalgam of MG and other Nuffield components, 'Bitsy' was a strange but purposeful-looking two-seater machine which, according to the magazine, used a 1,292cc TB engine (though one of those facts must be wrong – in fact it was a 1,250cc XPAG unit), but ran with a 7:1 final drive ratio! The radiator, incidentally, looked suspiciously like that of a 1920s-vintage 14/40 model.

It is difficult to see the direct ancestry of the chassis and suspension, because it used an incredibly short chassis with a wheelbase of 5ft 10in (1,778mm), which was 24in (610mm) shorter than that of the TA/TB. On the other hand, the wheeltracks were wider: *The Autocar* quoted these as 4ft 10in (1,491mm) – 13in (330mm) wider than those of the TB – but then stated that the axles and wheels were from the Magnette, whose track was 4ft 0in (1,219mm). Since no MG, and as far as I am aware no Morris or Wolseley ever used tracks so wide, I leave MG number-crunchers to work out what was wrong, and where! Centre-lock Magnette-type wire-spoke wheels were fitted, but with considerably over-sized tyres.

The body panelling was fitted to cover only the engine and the wheels themselves, and could best be described as 'skimpy': for this machine's purpose was solely as a tug, sometimes with up to three trailers in a 'train', and MG claimed that at one point it had actually moved 8½ tons in one particular operation. *The Autocar*'s H. S.

Linfield was ecstatic, describing the car as having:

> ... very big tyres, 'comps' on the rear, sketchy though adequately wide wings, no windscreen, no doors – in fact, no body! On a platform are two bucket seats, and that is the end of the amenities ... There has been no fussiness over details such as instruments: there isn't a single gauge!

Even though motoring for fun was officially discouraged by this time, there was still the opportunity to take the car out onto the rough tracks of the Berkshire Ridgeway:

> Over tracks, muddy and rutted, or hard-surfaced rough stuff, 'Bitsy' was even better than for ordinary driving. 'Open the throttle and hang on' would be the plan if you tackled a trials course in it. You would not have to pick a course, nor ease the throttle to minimize wheelspin, nor would you have the slightest doubt about power. The springs have that old-time hardness, so that you know very definitely when you have hit a bump or a hump – but nothing would deflect 'Bitsy' from its course. You could gauge things on corners to an inch at either side. In short, a trials secretary's terror.

In the gloomiest period of the conflict, this was just one way in which the MG workforce kept in touch with its heritage. By 1944, though, an end to that dreadful conflict was at last in sight: so how should MG plan for its future?

TB (1939 only)

Numbers built :
379
Production period : May 1939 – September 1939

Layout
Ladder-type separate steel chassis frame, with steel panelled body panels on a wooden bodyshell skeleton. Two-door, front engine/rear drive, sold as a two-seater open sports car, or as a two-seater Tickford-bodied drop-head coupe.

Engine

Type	Nuffield, Type XPAG
Block material	Cast iron
Head material	Cast iron
Cylinders	4 in-line
Cooling	Water
Bore and stroke	66.5 x 90mm
Capacity	1,250cc
Main bearings	3
Valves	2 per cylinder, operated by in-line overhead valves, pushrods and rockers, with camshaft mounted in block, driven by chain from crankshaft
Compression ratio	7.25:1
Carburettors	2 SU
Max. power	54bhp @ 5,200rpm
Max. torque	64lb ft @ 2,600rpm

Transmission
Four-speed manual gearbox, with synchromesh on top, third and second gears

Clutch	Single dry plate

Overall gearbox ratios

Top	5.125
3rd	6.92
2nd	10.0
1st	17.32
Reverse	17.32
Final drive	5.125:1 (spiral bevel)

15.84mph (25.49km/h)/1,000rpm in top gear

Suspension and steering

Front	Beam axle, half-elliptic leaf springs, Luvax hydraulic lever-arm dampers
Rear	Live (beam) axle, with half-elliptic leaf springs and Luvax hydraulic lever-arm dampers
Steering	Cam-gear
Tyres	4.50-19in cross-ply

Wheels	Centre-lock wire spoke
Rim width	2.5in

Brakes

Type	Drum brakes at front, drums at rear, hydraulically operated
Size	9 x 1.5in front and rear drums

Dimensions (in/mm)

Track	
Front	45/1143mm
Rear	45/1143mm
Wheelbase	94/2388mm
Overall length	139.75/3550mm
Overall width	56/1422mm
Overall height	
(hood erect)	53/1346mm
Unladen weight	1,765lb/800kg

UK retail price

2-seater Sports	£225
Tickford-bodied DHC	£270

4 TC: Abingdon's Export Success

Until 1944, in theory at least, with the war effort and military production at its height, no one in the British motor industry was supposed to be planning its post-war models. In theory, but not in fact. Most of its engineers, if not the top management, found time to think about their future, if only on paper and on the 'why don't we ...?' basis. It seems that MG, however, stuck loyally to its wartime efforts longer than most; and even though Nuffield's vice-chairman, Sir Miles Thomas, had encouraged Alec Issigonis to get on with the design of the Morris Minor by 1943, there

Saints and sinner? The Morris Minor of 1928 was the car which inspired the first MG Midgets, and Lord Nuffield (centre) set up the MG Car Co.; but it was Sir Miles Thomas (right) who eventually sacked Cecil Kimber in 1941.

didn't seem to be much interest in new MGs at that time. Early in 1945, however, MG managing director H. A. Ryder (who had taken over from Cecil Kimber in 1941) consulted Syd Enever and Cecil Cousins about post-war models. This occurred just before John Thornley returned to Abingdon, for during the war he had been commissioned in the RAOC, emerging with the rank of lieutenant colonel.

Clearly there was no way that brand-new MGs could be designed and put into production immediately. Ryder, who was on the main Nuffield board, had already been told that the SA/VA/WA types were not to be reintroduced, and the decision had also made to end MG's contract with Tickford for bodyshells, which inevitably meant that this left Abingdon ready to produce nothing but two-seater sports cars. But was it enough to start making TBs again, without change? If not, what changes could be made quickly, cheaply, and without complication? Many years after the event Cecil Cousins had this to say in an interview:

After the war we said: 'What will we make?' H. A. Ryder (our MD) said: 'Well, we'd better make the TB again.' And someone wisely said: 'Well, we'd better find out what's wrong with it.'

For its post-war customers, MG swiftly turned the TB Midget into this: the TC. Except that these cars had a black-painted grille, there was absolutely no change to the front-end style.

Compared with the TB, the TC had a slightly wider cockpit, which meant that changes were made to the body framing itself. Compared with later Midgets, the rear aspect of the TC was extremely simple.

So they went through the records to find out what items we had the biggest number of complaints on, and that sort of public criticism. The only two things that anyone could point to was that it [the TB: author] wasn't wide enough, and that the sliding shackles were the biggest service item. So they made the body four inches [10cm] wider across the cockpit, and replaced the sliding trunnions with rubber shackles to get over the other problem. And that was how the TC came to be.

BMIHT tell me that the original TC proto-type – probably the only TC prototype – carried the chassis number TC0251, and was probably the 1939–1940 TB demon-strator (CJB 59) which was reworked according to the decisions just described.

This, incidentally, was the very same TB which had been driven by *The Autocar* in 1940 (a test summarized in the previous chapter).

The TB was therefore consigned to the history books after a very short life, for the records confirm that it was only produced in 1939. Hindsight, however, is a wonderful thing, because developing the TC from the TB was not quite as simple as it sounds, and getting it into production was even less so.

EXTRA COCKPIT WIDTH

Every previous book about T-Series MGs has swallowed the party line that the post-war TC's cockpit was 4in (10cm) wider than that of the pre-war TA/TB variety, even though the overall width of the cars (4ft 8in/142cm) did not change, and nor did either the front or the rear wheeltrack dimensions. However, if only on the visual evidence, I have always been uneasy about this extra 4in, so this time, and to ease my doubts, I have researched a little further.

When the TC was launched in October 1945 the two 'establishment' magazines – *The Autocar* and *The Motor* – both quoted the magic extra-width figure of 4in (10cm), which makes it certain that this figure was detailed in MG's own press information. According to *The Motor*: 'Although similar in outline to TA and TB models, it is, in fact, four inches wider over the seat than the last named...'

Then I looked at the dimensions quoted in road tests, and found a rather different story: first, *The Autocar*'s TA road test of

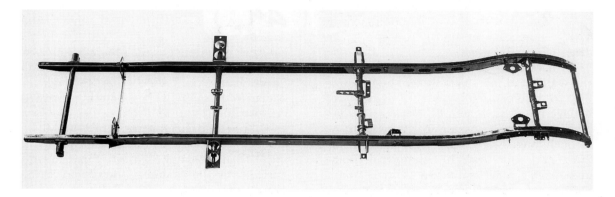

The TA/TB/TC chassis frame was simplicity itself. There are no battery cradles towards the back of this frame (left of the picture) which identifies it, therefore, as a TC item.

The rear end of the TC chassis differed from that of the TA/TB in detail, firstly by having shackles instead of trunnions for the rear mounting of the leaf springs, and because the electrical batteries were no longer placed ahead of the back axle.

1936 includes a carefully dimensioned drawing of the bodyshell, showing a maximum cockpit width of 41 3/4in (106cm) just behind the line of the seats – and in fact this might not even have been the widest point of the cockpit. Across the facia panel, just ahead of the seats, the width was less, at 39 1/2in (100cm). Then in 1947 *The Autocar* tested a TC, this time quoting 44in (112cm) across the seat cushion, and 41in (104cm) across the facia panel. That's an increase of just over 2in (5cm) – not 4in. (*The Motor*'s test of a TC, published in 1947, is not as informative, nor are the drawings as detailed.)

So according to MG press information, the width had increased by 4in; but according to independent measurement (and, believe me, I have actually witnessed such measurements being taken, very carefully, by such magazine testers) it was only about 2in (5cm). Not that this changes history, and it isn't very significant – but I would still like to know who exaggerated what had been achieved, and why? In any case, the increase in cockpit width was limited by the overall width of the car itself, and by the fact that changes had to be made at the Morris Bodies branch to the body framing and skin panels, and to where (and how) they were to be fixed to the sweep of the wings and the running board. This, no doubt, explains why the first 'off-track' TC wasn't actually produced until 17 September 1945, four months after the end of the war in Europe.

Besides, the planners at the Morris Bodies branch of Coventry, which had been badly bombed in 1940, took time to reorganize the plant for peacetime production – indeed it is a miracle that their stored bodyshell tooling had not been destroyed. Although the extra 4in (or 2in ... make up your own minds) might sound minor to you, it also involved making changes to the scuttle/bulkhead, the floor, the doors themselves, and to the panelling surrounding the soft-top stowage area.

This wasn't the only change to the bodyshell: hidden away on the TA and TB, 12-volt electricity had been provided by two small 6-volt batteries, wired in series, each mounted in a small pressed steel cradle in the chassis, at each side and just ahead of the line of the rear axle. Now, for the TC model, there was to be a larger, 12-volt battery, positioned in a box on the front bulkhead, just behind and above the engine.

Other mechanical changes were confined to the suspension, which was to be just as hard-sprung as before, but better controlled and probably longer-lasting. Instead of the sliding trunnion fixings at the rear end of the four leaf springs, which had to be greased regularly to allow the spring to move freely, though slightly, forward and back in its alloy casting, there were to be conventional shackles.

At the rear this was done by cropping the rear cross-member of the frame, welding a shackle pivot in place below the line of the original trunnion, and arranging for the swinging shackle to be placed above that pivot, with the spring/shackle junction almost (but not quite) in the same position as before. The suspension geometry, therefore, was really unaffected.

By the time MG had retrieved all its assembly facilities from the St Helen's factory in Abingdon, and a small supply of every other component had been secured, the summer of 1945 was over, which meant that the very first 'off-tools' TC was not produced until mid-September. Even then, the production build-up was agonizingly slow, because only eighty-one new cars were released in the next three months (100 were built, but there was a small lag between completion and despatch). This

Luvax hydraulic lever-arm dampers were fitted on TC models, their position on the frame being unchanged.

This was the TC rolling chassis, prior to having its bodyshell fitted. Note the new position for the 12-volt battery, on the bulkhead immediately behind the engine.

was nothing to be ashamed about, for every British car-maker was suffering from the same shortages and delays – and not only of parts, but of personnel, too. MG, like other companies, had to wait for many of their workers to be demobilized from the Forces; and some of them, tragically, would never return.

Forty-seven of those cars – more than half of total production – were allocated to the export market, this setting a trend which was to intensify in the next few years. Times had changed a great deal and, quite simply, 'Britain Ltd' was economically so exhausted by the war that it needed to export as much as possible, as rapidly as possible, to try to get back on terms. Before the war, MG had been happy to satisfy the home market while sending a few cars to overseas markets. Now, although there was a huge demand for cars at home, a rigidly applied government licencing system meant that few TCs could initially be allocated to British customers. Even so, there would never be any left-hand-drive TCs...

One result of the war was that there had been considerable inflation, which meant that costs (of components and of labour) had risen considerably. This, and the fact that the government was now imposing a $33 \frac{1}{3}$ per cent purchase tax on the ex-works wholesale price of every new car, made the jump between British TB and TC prices look astronomical:

Even after six years of war, however, there were no changes to the 'cottage-industry' assembly methods at Abingdon. Once the simple ladder-style chassis frame was 'dressed' and ready, it formed its own assembly jig for the rest of the car. Front beam axles came in from a supplier, rear axles from a Nuffield subsidiary, and once the springs, 19in wheels and tyres had all been added, the assembly was ready to be pushed slowly along the assembly channels for other major items to be added.

The XPAG engine and its related four-speed gearbox arrived from Coventry, ready for dropping into place, and the entire rolling chassis would then be sprayed black before the body was bolted into place. In the meantime, other transporters delivered the ready-painted two-seater bodyshell centre section from the Morris Bodies branch, also of Coventry, though the folding bonnet pressings and the flowing front wings had to be specially fitted, adjusted and fettled before they would match the radiator block.

Each and every TC was then road-tested – on the open road, however briefly, and traditionally on the Marcham Road to the west of the town – before it left the factory for its customer.

TC ON THE MARKET

For the first few years, at least, the TC's

Model	Retail price	Purchase tax	Total price (including tax)
1939 TB	£225	-	£225
1945 TC	£375	£105	£480

The TC and the British Market Place

The TC of 1945 was a lightly modified 1939-style TB, and it was the very first British sports car to go back on sale after World War II. Most 1930s rivals had dropped out of the picture, so apart from the tiny HRG concern, by mid-1947 the TC's obvious British competitors were:

HRG (1,074cc)	£812.14
HRG (1,496cc)	£967.55
MG TC (1,250cc)	**£527.83**
Morgan 4/4 (1,267cc)	£524.00
Singer Nine Roadster (1,074cc)	£511.86

(The imposition of Purchase Tax had boosted prices considerably since 1939.)

The HRG was far too expensive to make any impression, while Morgan production was limited, as it had been in the 1930s. The Singer Roadster was not nearly as sporty as the TC, being heavier, slower and less nimble. Faced with this poor crop of British rivals, it would have been easy for MG to have become complacent.

All TCs had right-hand drive, even those exported in large numbers to the USA, and they were bodied as two-seater roadsters. The engine exhaust silencer, please note, was placed directly under the driver's seat: unofficial heating!

The TC's facia/instrument layout, so characteristic of all the Midgets made at Abingdon in the 1930s and 1940s. It is an interesting study in priorities: thus although there is a clock (inset to the rev-counter, ahead of the driver's eyes), there are no gauges to register fuel contents or water temperature.

future was assured, as the shortages and write-offs of war had ensured a world-wide demand for new cars of any type. Because tens of thousands of virile young men had been posted to the UK during World War II, and 1930s-style MGs had been freely usable to those with access to petrol, their reputation spread all over the world. We don't know how many survivors of that awful conflict took MGs home with them after the fighting had stopped, but it seems certain that thousands took back memories which were never to fade. If you don't believe me, take a careful note of the cars which figure so strongly in the patriotic war films of the period, and of the immediate post-war years....

Even though official exports of TCs to the USA did not begin until the end of 1947, I am convinced that MG's reputation in North America preceded it. For the first time specialist motoring magazines concen-

trating on 'imports' were set up, and the marque's exposure mushroomed.

If it had not needed to supply certain markets to comply with British government edicts, the fact is that for some considerable time MG could have sold as many TCs as it could possibly put together. But the British government of the day had built up a virulently anti-motoring legislation: initially there was a strictly enforced licensing scheme which limited the sale of new cars to 'essential users', and this was soon joined by a 'covenant' scheme which forbade the quick sale of new cars by their first owners, who might have been out to make a profit; because of this the waiting lists grew longer and longer here at home, while more cars were sent overseas than ever before.

Early in 1946, about 110 to 120 TC sports cars were being produced every month, and though this was not as many as the TA/TB cars had reached at their peak, in those shortage-ridden days it was a miracle. In 1947, by which time the various supply problems were beginning to ease, that figure had been pushed up to around 150 to 160 cars a month; and if MG could have found more parts, and if more investment in production facilities could have been made, those figures might even have increased. For those lucky drivers who could buy new TCs, everything about the car spelt out 'sports car' – or should I say, 'traditional sports car'. Except in its price and – marginally – in its performance (for post-war petrol, being low-octane 'pool', was a poor relation to the best quality 1930s supplies), the TC was still pure 1930s.

So, what if the styling was much the same as it had been for more than ten years? And what if the ride was hard, the steering heavy at low speeds, and the weather protection not perfect? This was an MG, and this was a sports car. Not only that, but the TC reminded almost everyone that although the 1940s might be dull, drab and depressing, the 1930s had been rather different! It was not only the sight, but the sound, the smell and the character of the car which as a whole harked back to more peaceful, placid days.

In the late 1940s not only was it wonderful to have a sports car at all, it was of course great to be alive. No one who came out of the fire, blast and horror of the 1939 –1945 conflict worried too much about trends, nor complained about obsolescence: he was just happy to have his freedom, his smell of fresh air with the top down, and his own fun. The motoring press, at least, were happy to see that MG had recovered so rapidly from the war; they were delighted to welcome a new model of MG, were happy to see that the TC was selling so

Even though the TC had its battery mounted up front, on the bulkhead, there was still enough space around the XPAG engine to allow individual owners to do their own maintenance. The diagonal stiffening bars between the radiator and the bulkhead were removable.

Except for the repositioned battery box (the voltage regulator is fixed to that box), there was no difference between the TB (see Chapter 3) and this, the TC under-bonnet installation.

well, and were often pleased to confirm that, in their opinion, Britain was still best.

The Motor tested a TC (registered DBL 606) in April 1947, headlining its report : 'A Sports Car in the Traditional Style'. Noting a maximum speed of 73mph (117km/h), with 0–60mph (0–96km/h) acceleration in 21.1sec, the testers wrote as follows:

> The TC-type MG two-seater is essentially a sports car in the traditional style, and following a prolonged spell of sedate motoring in a family saloon of equivalent h.p., initial mileage on it necessitates a rapid readjustment of reactions and outlook...
>
> ...the acceleration on the indirect speeds is such that most other cars can be left behind when the lights go green.
>
> Suspension on the TC-type is completely orthodox, with short semi-elliptics at front and rear controlled by Luvax piston-type shock absorbers. This combination, coupled with a rigid frame, provides a very solid feeling and results in good stability at speed.
>
> Short of fitting remote-control shock absorbers – and one would scarcely expect to find these as a standard fitment on what is, after all, the cheapest sports car on the market today – it is difficult with such orthodox springing layout to arrive at a suspension which gives truly satisfactory results throughout the whole range ... at speeds below 40mph [64km/h], except on roads with an impeccable surface, the ride becomes increasingly harsh as the speed diminishes...

In summary *The Motor* was impressed, but did not seem to be overwhelmed:

> To sum up, the TC-type MG provides a very adequate means of transport for those who place performance and stability and an ability to go almost anywhere, high on their list of requirements. Mechanical accessibility is above average, and by present-day standards the car represents very good value at the all-in price of £527 16s 8d.

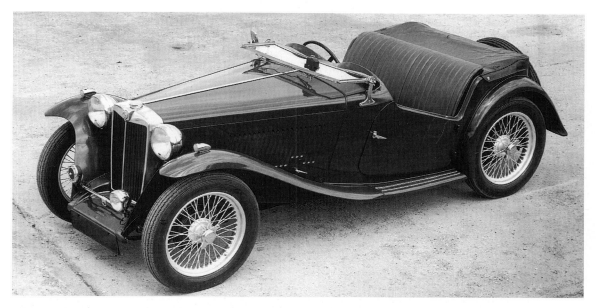

Already familiar to British customers, the TA/TB/TC style would also be seen in the United States from the late 1940s. By 1930s standards there isn't a line or a detail out of place.

TC assembly at Abingdon in 1946. This chassis was at the very beginning of the simple assembly line, where cars were pushed forwards from station to station. The engine/gearbox assembly is just about to be craned into place.

Just before the government withdrew the last drops of 'private' petrol from the British market, *The Autocar* tested the same TC in October 1947 – sublimely commemorating what should have been Motor Show week in London! – and were obviously delighted with DBL 606's traditional character:

Today it is certainly a class alone among cars made anywhere in the world: thus as a sporting type it retains the conventional outward appearance of a 'real' car dear to the hearts of enthusiasts in years gone by – that is, by displaying its radiator, or at all events a normal grille, and lamps, and in not having gone 'all streamlined'... And yet no car has done so much to maintain open-air motoring, and to support the demand that exists all over the world for sports car performance and characteristics in a car of not exorbitant first cost, and maintainable at moderate running costs.

It offers a great deal in sheer performance ... The Midget is in no way more difficult to drive than the ordinary family saloon, but given the type of driver who usually falls for such a machine – not necessarily a youngster – and one who likes to use the gearbox, the performance becomes quite vivid.

Owing to its handy size, its ability to pass safely where a bigger car would be held back, and the way in which it regains its cruising rate after it has been checked by other traffic, the Midget is almost as fast a car over British roads as can be found today.

HVC 501 was often used in MG TC publicity pictures in the late 1940s. The girls – Abingdon staff, maybe? – are in the very best of 1940s fashion, too.

Its handiness, the way in which it helps the driver in its manner of cornering, and its 'quick' steering, are big factors in giving it unusual average speed capabilities without an extremely high maximum speed being attained.

Even though the TC had extremely hard suspension, *The Autocar* was ready to make allowances for that:

The merits and demerits of normal versus independent suspension can be argued, in the main to the latter's marked advantage; but there is no doubt of one fact in this connection, and that is that the normally sprung car, rather hard sprung, as in this instance, does let the driver gauge within close limits the speeds at which he can cor-

ner safely fast. After a little experience of it one finds oneself holding quite high speeds round bends in the Midget, and the car steering to a close course only a foot or two out from the near-side verge. Such a half-elliptic suspension has, of course, the counterbalancing feature that it is on the harsh side over poor surfaces...

Performance figures are quoted in detail on page 180, this particular TC having a top speed of 75mph (137km/h), with 0–60mph (0–97km/h) in 22.7 seconds. Both of the 'establishment' magazines had therefore achieved similar performance figures to the TA, which seems to confirm that the extra power of the XPAG engine (which was originally measured on high-quality 1939 petrol) had almost exactly been negated by

Delicious posed shot of a batch of six TCs being delivered to a police force. Good for a giggle, no doubt, and able to outhandle almost every other car on British roads – but where would the police store any of its gear?

the use of low-octane 'pool' petrol.

Looking back, it is easy to say that MG should have replaced the TC with a more forward-looking design much earlier than in fact it did, but this is to ignore the realities of the post-war situation. Competition to the TC was no stronger than it had been for the TA/TB models in the late 1930s, and MG's own distribution and dealer organization was much superior to that of any rival. For the first few years the TC's only direct competition in the smaller-engined sports-car market came from HRG, Morgan and Singer, none of whom were making cars in significant numbers, and none of which had any technical, performance or commercial advantages: at this time, HRG was building just one car a week, and Morgan two or three, while the Singer Roadster, though popular, was a four-seater roadster rather than a two-seater sports car. In effect the TC therefore had the true small-engined sports car market to itself, and it was going to take years before any rival could match, let alone surpass this position.

Thus it was that until 1947 the Abingdon workforce could concentrate on building the TC, and no other model; the first of the new Y-Type saloons was not announced until May of that year, and the very first Riley RM-Series models would not be added to Abingdon's output until 1949. In actual fact the problem was more one of supply than of demand. For MG, the great news was that the TC was becoming popular all over the world, and even though serious deliveries of cars to the USA did not begin until 1948, word was obviously getting around. And holiday trips like that reported in *The Autocar* of 20 June 1947 must surely have added to interest in the United States: Flt Lt John Bentley took his newly run-in TC from New York City to Indianapolis, and back to New York – 1,435 miles (2,309km) in five days, which included a two-stay stopover in Indianapolis itself.

To Americans, who were already taking delivery of large pre-war design Fords, Chevrolets and the like, the TC must have looked like a toy, but it never seemed to be struggling to keep up with the flow. Excerpts from the log included: 'First 55 miles of Turnpike in 1hr 5min. Overtaking a 6-wheel truck doing 70mph. Battle with a Dodge saloon car – passed him at over 80mph.'

At other points the crew recorded an indicated top speed of 83mph (134km/h) and passed a truck-plus-trailer which was itself clocking 78mph (126km/h).

In the meantime, TCs had started appearing all over the world, not in large numbers, but in many different countries. Amazingly, Argentina was Nuffield's most successful export market in 1945, with ten cars, while six cars went to Eire (the Irish Republic); however, those were not representative, as 1946 was to prove. That was the year in which 638 MGs were sent abroad, a figure which included 108 to Australia, 83 to Southern Africa, 70 to Argentina, 59 to Switzerland and 49 to India/Pakistan (nations which had not, at that time, been separated). But only twenty cars to the USA and six to Canada.

Then, according to figures extracted from Nuffield Exports statistics, the flood of MG exports to North America began. In 1947 a total of 234 cars went to the USA, and in 1948 no fewer than 1,143 would follow. Twenty cars went to Canada in 1947, and 247 in 1948. These included all the Y-Types, however, so the following table, which concerns only TCs, tells a slightly different story. The important development to note, though, was the way that exports built up in the five years the TC was being built:

	1945	1946	1947	1948	1949
Home market cars	34	1,001	1,146	297	930
Export market, RHD	47	638	1,194	1,278	1,340
Export, North America	0	0	6	1,473	522
Chassis only, RHD	0	0	0	1	9
CKD cars	0	36	0	36	12
Total	81	1,675	2,346	3,085	2,813

This confirms that only 2,001 cars – just 20 per cent of the TC total – were exported to North America, which nullifies the assertion that the only reason for TC sales figures being so good was because most of the cars were sent to that vast continent. Amazingly, in spite of the manifold restrictions which the British government placed on the selling of new cars at home, more than one third of all TCs were delivered here. The TC's export success, however, was largely due to the great reception accorded to the sports car in the traditional 'British Empire' countries, especially Australia and Southern Africa, though many were also taken by countries as far flung as Malaya, Argentina, Hong Kong, India/Pakistan and Brazil.

SPECIAL TCs FOR NORTH AMERICA

Faced with high demand from North America (and pressure from the dealers), the Cowley design office re-worked the basic design of the TC so as to make it more suitable for the dense traffic and more robust driving conditions of that continent – though, strangely, this derivative was never produced in left-hand-drive form. I have always been puzzled by this, for many other Nuffield cars were certainly redesigned to accept left-hand drive at this time; Charles Griffin, later to become a very exalted engineer in BMC and British Leyland, was personally involved in that on-going process.

Except that the TC was quite a slim car (which meant that the driver would not have to move his eye line very far to get a good view along the flanks of another LHD car), the only reason I can suggest is that a left-hand-drive installation might actually have been extremely difficult to arrange. On the standard right-hand-drive car, the steering column passed through the engine bay, close to the right side of the cylinder block. If a left-hand-drive column had passed through the engine bay, to the left-side of the block, would the oil pump and filter bodies have got in the way? Whatever the reason, no attempt was ever made to produce LHD TCs, in spite of the mistaken identification of 168 such cars in Abingdon's surviving records!

A dedicated USA-market TC was eventually developed, with despatches beginning at the end of 1948. Although the cars were still only made with right-hand-drive, and had no significant mechanical changes, they had extra equipment to make them more suitable for North American roads. Added to the basic specification were front and rear bumpers (have you ever seen a photograph? I am afraid I have not been able to trace one); twin and quite melodious Lucas 'Windtone' horns; and twin tail lamps. Flashing direction indicator bulbs were incorporated in the front side-lamps, and in the relocated tail-lamps.

The first of these cars carried chassis no. 7380, a machine built in December 1948, which according to the records means that approximately 700 such cars eventually crossed the Atlantic. Statistics, of course, can be made to prove many things, but there is evidence that the Americans' passion for the TC was already cooling at this time, for MG's 1949 exports of USA-market TCs were only one third of the 1948 figures. In this assertion I am not trying to undermine the TC's reputation or its obvious success in the USA, but am merely stating the facts – and am suggesting that the Nuffield dealer network in North America might have ordered too many TCs in 1948. For some time in 1949, therefore, two versions of the TC must have been on sale in North America, the 'normal' and the 'USA-version' types, side by side.

UNREPEATABLE CHARACTER

By mid-1949 the TC's career was drawing to a close, thus bringing to an end the original statement of 'Abingdon engineering' which had been laid down nearly twenty years earlier. Even before they studied the brochures or sat in a car, by this time customers knew exactly what sort of motoring they would get from a Midget. Not that sales were falling away: in 1948, 250 to 280 TCs had been built in an average month, the highest level so far achieved by any MG model, and that level of production would be maintained until the autumn of 1949. In the spring, when every enthusiast's mind was turning to the idea of open air motoring, MG produced 297 cars in March, 236 in April, 287 in May and 269 in June. This, along with the transfer of Riley assembly into the plant, made Abingdon a bustling and definitely profitable factory.

In performance, if not in character, the T-Series cars which had seemed fast in the 1930s were now beginning to struggle a little against post-war competition. A top speed of 75mph (120km/h) – or more reasonably, a cruising speed of 60mph (96km/h) – was no longer outstanding.

It was in its character, though, that the TC made so many positive statements. Although the ride, though somewhat softer than that of the J2 and PA/PB types, was still hard, this was what MG thought its public wanted. The steering was quite heavy – although the use of narrow tyres, with only limited tread widths, minimized this – but it was extremely direct, and made the car very 'chuckable'.

To own and enjoy a TC, though, meant accepting certain conditions: blissful to many buyers, purgatory to the few unbelievers who ever tried one – my own TA, when twenty years old, sent out the same messages as when it was new. To own a TA/TB/TC was to enjoy motoring for motoring's sake, with a very real sensation of speed, glamour, and close encounter with the countryside. As American billboard advertising once claimed for the TC: 'Driving is Fun Again!' A TC looked good, felt wonderful, and was a positive phallic invitation to be driven hard, and fast. As

Final assembly of TCs at Abingdon, circa 1947, with the newly launched Y-Type saloon taking shape on a parallel track. Almost every car in this line-up carries a 'Nuffield Export' sticker on its windscreen.

for comfort, warmth, peace and dignity – no, not really.

Comfortable enough on smooth main roads, a TC could be very hard work and tiring on bumpy surfaces. MG did not offer a heater, not even as an option, so the cockpit could get very cold in winter, especially if the floorboards and seals no longer fitted closely together. Original-condition hood and sidescreens gave reasonable weather protection, but there was still a tendency for driving rain to find its way in somehow, from somewhere – not for nothing did trials drivers tend to don motorcycle-standard clothing to enjoy their sport.

Although none of this had mattered when the design was new, it increasingly began to be significant in the late 1940s. For the 1950s, and especially for sale in the USA, MG knew that they needed a new model – and the TD was the result.

FALSE START: HOW NOT TO REPLACE THE TC

Before the TD eventually took over from the TC, a great deal of manoeuvring took place along the way. In the main, this revolved around the Cowley design offices, their desire to maintain total authority over Abingdon, and their thoughts on squeezing new variants from the brand-new Morris Minor design.

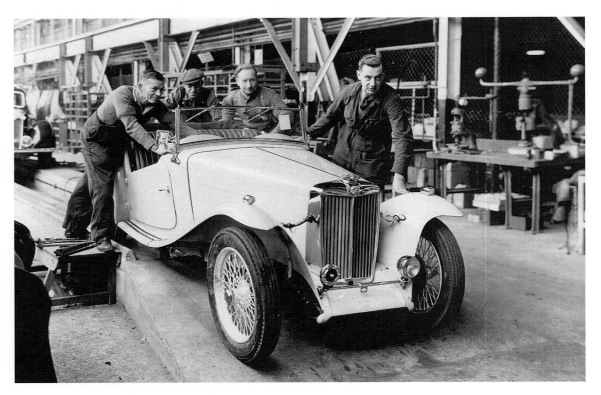

The end of an era, as the very last TC is pushed off the assembly line at Abingdon in 1949. Not only was this the last TC, it was also the last beam-front-axle car ever to be built at Abingdon.

This is a complicated story which I will keep very brief. Alec Issigonis began the design of the Morris Minor in 1942, the project was ready for production by 1947, and after some delay the new model was launched in October 1948. Adding to the intrigue was the fact that Sir Miles Thomas, Nuffield's vice-chairman who eventually walked away from Cowley at the end of 1947, was the Minor's most important backer, whilst Lord Nuffield himself hated its looks ('a bloody poached egg' is what he thought of the style).

Known at Cowley at first as the 'Mosquito', the new Minor used a new unit construction shell with independent front suspension by torsion bars, and with rack-and-pinion steering. The production engine was an uninspired Morris Engines Branch 918cc unit. At the prototype stage Cowley planners then proposed to develop an 'MG1100' version of the saloon, which would have had an overhead-valve (Wolseley 8-type) version of that engine, and which might have been assembled at Cowley. This never got beyond the 'good-idea/mock-up' stage, however, and was stillborn.

Then came the DO926 project, tentatively badged as the MG 'Midget Major', which combined the Morris Minor floorpan, and a new 1.1-litre overhead-cam Wolseley engine which only existed as a paper project. This, I must make it clear, was all Cowley's idea, and I doubt if anyone at Abingdon (most especially George Propert, who had been MG's most senior resident manager after Cecil Kimber was sacked) was even consulted about it. DO926/'Midget Major' was mocked up, full size, in 1947 and 1948, shown both as a two-seater drop-head or with the alternative of a hardtop panel. As far as I can see, no running prototype was ever completed.

This was also the time when MG and Riley became embroiled in a Nuffield rationalization proposal. At management level there was battle royal, for it was proposed that one set of assembly lines should be moved to the other factory – and at one point there was a very real chance that MG assembly would be moved to the Riley factory in Coventry! Fortunately Nuffield decided to relocate Riley assembly at Abingdon, rather than the other way round, which pleased Propert enormously, and encouraged him to retire in mid-1949, a happy and contented MG man who had seen great traditions preserved.

Once the 'Midget Major' project had been shelved (no physical trace of it remains, though a few pictures survive), the way was clear for Abingdon to make its own proposals for a TC replacement. The result was the TD of 1950, which would be MG's best-seller so far.

TC (1945 – 1949)

Numbers built
10,000
Production period: September 1945 – November 1949

Layout
Ladder-type separate steel chassis frame, with steel panelled body panels on a wooden bodyshell skeleton. Two-door, front engine/rear drive, sold as two-seater open sports car.

Engine

Type	Nuffield, Type XPAG
Block material	Cast iron
Head material	Cast iron
Cylinders	4 in-line
Cooling	Water
Bore and stroke	66.5 x 90mm
Capacity	1,250cc
Main bearings	3
Valves	2 per cylinder, operated by in-line overhead valves, pushrods and rockers, with camshaft mounted in block, driven by chain from crankshaft
Compression ratio	7.25:1
Carburettors	2 SU
Max. power	54bhp @ 5,200rpm
Max. torque	64lb ft @ 2,600rpm

Transmission
Four-speed manual gearbox, with synchromesh on top, third and second gears

Clutch	Single dry plate

Overall gearbox ratios

Top	5.125
3rd	6.92
2nd	10.0
1st	17.32
Reverse	17.32
Final drive	5.125:1 (spiral bevel)

15.84mph (25.49km/h)/1,000rpm in top gear

Suspension and steering

Front	Beam axle, half-elliptic leaf springs, Luvax hydraulic lever-arm dampers
Rear	Live (beam) axle, with half-elliptic leaf springs and Luvax hydraulic lever-arm dampers
Steering	Cam-gear
Tyres	4.50-19in cross-ply
Wheels	Centre-lock wire spoke
Rim width	2.5in

Brakes

Type	Drum brakes at front, drums at rear, hydraulically operated
Size	9 x 1.5in front and rear drums

Dimensions (in/mm)

Track	
Front	45/1,143mm
Rear	45/1,143mm
Wheelbase	94/2,388mm
Overall length	139.75/3,550mm
Overall width	56/1,422mm
Overall height	
(hood erect)	53/1,346mm
Unladen weight	1,735lb/787kg

UK retail price

At launch in 1945:	£479.92 (basic price £375)
From mid-1946:	£527.83 (basic price £412.50)

USA retail price

In 1948	$2,238
In 1949	$2,395

5 TD: New Engineering, Old Style

Cast your minds back fifty years, to the late 1940s: MG was selling sports cars – TCs – as fast as it could make them. The world was at peace, and war-torn economies were recovering fast; young people were looking for a bit of fun, and a new sports car was on their list. So far so good, but for MG there

was already a cloud on the horizon: even though it did not yet face modern competition, the TC was beginning to look old-fashioned. By 1949, and by any previous Abingdon standards, it was ages since MG had produced a new Midget, and so it would not be long before a new car – let us

John Thornley (left) and Syd Enever were two of the most important characters to influence the birth and development of the TD and TF models. Thornley would eventually stay at MG until 1969, and Enever until 1971.

90

call it the TD – had to be developed. In any case, there was a restless air of change at Abingdon and Cowley. Not only had the Riley RM-Series assembly been moved from Coventry to Abingdon (no one actually mentioned the phrase 'cuckoo in the nest', but it was certainly apt...), but there had been a wholesale change of management at Nuffield.

Although Cowley's design team was still intact, Sir Miles Thomas's departure (Nuffield's vice-chairman until the end of 1947) had handed over executive power to Reg Hanks, while the reputation of Vic Oak's technical staff was now bolstered by Alec Issigonis (who had grown famous because of the excellence of the new Morris Minor) and Gerald Palmer, the designer of the Jowett Javelin, who had recently been made responsible for MG and Riley innovations.

A NEW MIDGET: WHICH WAY?

In 1949 the Nuffield Organization was still independent of any other car-maker, and proud of it. Lord Nuffield, technically if not commercially out of his depth since the 1930s, allowed Hanks to impose further rationalization on the business, though there is little evidence that either of them was thinking much about MG at this time, or what should be done about its future. Down the road at Abingdon, 'Pop' Propert, John Thornley and Syd Enever had plenty of their own ideas, which could be summarized in one sentence: to keep Cowley influence out of the place at all costs! They considered that in the last decade there had been quite enough destructive interference into MG's affairs, and they wanted to be rid of it.

Although a new Midget was certainly needed, for a time there was no evidence that the Cowley design office knew what do, or even cared very much about it. Earlier efforts to produce a sporting tourer from the basis of the YA saloon, the YT Tourer, were mundane in the extreme, while any combination of 'Morris Midget' or 'Midget Major' had filled Abingdon with horror. Gerald Palmer, who knew all about sports cars (he had designed a very smart little prototype of his own in the late 1930s), was really far too busy with new saloon car projects to get involved. Every time that Propert told Reg Hanks that MG needed a new-model Midget now, not later, he was apparently told that Cowley could not provide either the people or the time to the job. In the end, S. V. Smith, one of

---

Building the Cars: the Abingdon Factory

Although at first Abingdon was exclusively a factory for assembling MGs, that situation changed after World War II. From late 1957 it also became the home of the Austin-Healey marque, and even before that several different Riley models were assembled there too. During the life of the T-Series, the following cars were also produced at Abingdon:

Riley RM Series ($1\frac{1}{2}$-litre)
Riley RM Series ($2\frac{1}{2}$-litre)
Riley Pathfinder

After the T-Series had gone, Abingdon also embraced assembly of Riley 1.5s, Riley 2.6s and even of Morris Minor Travellers and Morris Minor vans.

The MG coil-spring independent front suspension, as first seen under the YA saloon, later in the TD, was designed by Alec Issigonis in the late 1930s. This intriguing workshop study shows a prototype installation actually fitted to a unit-construction Morris 10 car of that period.

technical chief Vic Oak's closest associates, suggested that if Abingdon was so keen, they should do the job themselves. And because of the way that Nuffield continued to rationalize its operations, he might also have added: 'And by the way, whatever you suggest must also use engines, transmissions and suspension parts which are already in production.' As always, time and scarce resources were working against MG.

No single person has ever claimed responsibility for what happened next, though Cecil Cousins, John Thornley, Syd Enever, Alec Hounslow and Henry Stone must all have been involved. The facts, though, are clear: that within two weeks a rather crudely mocked up two-seater machine had been cobbled together and sent up the road to Cowley with 'Something like that' hung around a headlamp!

The product planning of what became the TD went something like this:

1. Starting from the basis of the TC, what do we need?

A more modern chassis, independent front suspension, and more accurate steering.

A more up-to-date style.

A car to be built in right-hand or left-hand drive.

2. What must we retain?

The Abingdon touch. Safety Fast engineering. The TC's character. Developments of the TC's running gear.

Put like that, it sounds simple enough, but the team had to ask themselves these questions, too:

Will Cowley back our project?

What will the dealers (particularly in the USA) think?

Can we make it at a profit?

It was in this atmosphere, therefore, that

Syd Enever: Legendary Designer (1907 – 1993)

Syd Enever's most redoubtable claim to fame was his work on the MGAs and MGBs which followed the T-Series models; nevertheless he was an ever-present influence at Abingdon from 1921 to 1971. Hampshire-born, Enever's first job was as an errand boy at Morris Garages, then during the 1920s he made a big impression on Cecil Kimber, joining MG just before the move from Edmund Road (Cowley) to Abingdon.

At Abingdon he started as an experimental development engineer, and after MG design was forcibly moved to Cowley in 1935 he stayed at Abingdon in an engineering liaison role. After World War II he became increasingly prominent, working on TD and TF development as well as looking after the design of EX172 (the 1951 TD-based Le Mans car) and EX175 (the TD-powered prototype which was the true ancestor of the MGA). When the design office at Abingdon was officially re-opened in 1954, Syd became chief engineer, a position he held until he retired in 1971.

To quote my good friend and historian Jonathan Wood: 'Syd Enever was one of those quiet, intuitive engineers who delighted in jotting ideas down on scraps of paper and the backs of cigarette packets.'

Syd often attended MG gatherings, well into old age, and was a much respected member of the Abingdon fraternity.

MG's tiny experimental shop got working, and in a mere two weeks the 'good idea' was turned into reality. According to authoritative lists which have survived, there was never a special MG 'EX' code for this work, and the Cowley project code of DO968 was issued later, when re-engineering of the chassis and drawings for the bodyshell were being prepared!

Starting on the basis of the existing Cowley-designed YA saloon chassis – which not only had independent front suspension, but also used existing Nuffield/MG engine, transmission and back axle – the team shortened the wheelbase of this frame by 5in (127mm), substituted a TC-type engine for the single-carburettor engine normally to be found in the YA, then hurriedly fitted a modified TC bodyshell onto this frame. Because the Y-Type chassis had wider tracks and smaller/fatter wheels than the TC, it wasn't beautiful, it wasn't totally practical, and there wasn't even a day's driving or development in it, but at least it showed the way that Abingdon wanted a new Midget to be.

Forewarned that the lash-up was not at all like the car Abingdon hoped it should be, the engineers at Cowley looked at this odd-looking machine, granted a couple more weeks for it to be turned into something which looked better, took on board the logic, invented the DO968 code, and started work. In *MG by McComb*, Wilson McComb rather sniffily pointed out that: 'It must have looked most peculiar ... In due course Cowley brought out the finished TD design on this basis.'

Working around the parameters of the lash-up, chassis design was carried out at Cowley by Jack Daniels (who shortly before had been responsible for interpreting Issigonis's ideas for the Morris Minor), while body design was overseen by Jim O'Neill. Compared with the TC, whose chassis frame was narrow and none-too-rigid, the TD's frame was totally different, and relied on the bare bones of the Y-Type saloon's layout, including the front suspension and rear axle beam. Although the wheelbase dimension of the TC – 94in (2,388mm) – was retained, the wheeltracks

The Y-Type saloon, which had been designed in the late 1930s, was not actually introduced until 1947. Different in every way from the TC Midget, the Y-Type featured a sturdy box-section chassis frame, complete with independent front suspension. The TD Midget frame would eventually evolve from this.

This 'exploded' drawing shows the original Y-type chassis frame layout, complete with the coil-spring independent front suspension, along with rack-and-pinion steering, both of which would be used in the TD of 1950.

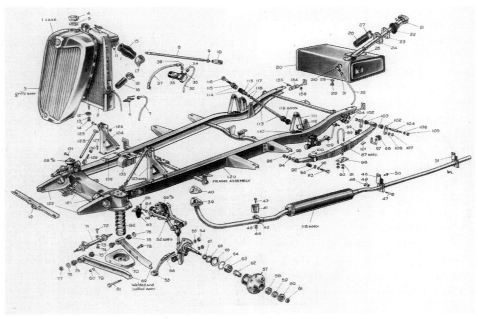

were significantly wider than before, particularly at the rear.

Although the TD's frame used the Y-Type frame as its inspiration, particularly in the box-section side members and the way it cradled the new-type independent front suspension, almost every pressing was different. Compared with the Y-Type, the major change was at the rear, where the TD's frame was swept up and over the line of the rear axle. Not only did this provide for more rear-axle bump movement, which meant that the suspension could be softened considerably, it also represented a real break in tradition. The J2 Midget of 1932 had used an 'underslung' chassis frame (in other words, the side members were under the line of the back axle), as

had all succeeding Midgets, and also the Y-Type.

To bring the design of the Midget thoroughly up to date, MG wanted to see independent front suspension used in the new TD, and were pleased to note that the system fitted to the Y-Type was already a success. With very few changes – notably to spring and damper settings – it was adopted for the TD, and basically it was so good that it would also be used on the TF, the MGA and the MGB which followed. Nuffield's original coil-spring/wishbone independent front suspension had been conceived at Cowley in the late 1930s by Alec Issigonis. Proposed, at first, for use in the Morris 10 Series M (which was announced in October 1938), it had been

The new coil-spring suspension, plus rack-and-pinion steering, as installed in the TD chassis, would become very familiar to MG owners, enthusiasts and garage mechanics in the next thirty years, for it was to be used in further developed form to the end of MGB production in 1980.

shunted sideways because of its cost. Later the same system had been reinstated for use in the MG Y-Type saloon, whose original launch was postponed because of the outbreak of war, and which finally went on sale in 1947.

Simple, compact, rigid and (as we later found out) very durable, this new suspension transformed the ride of the Midget. Right from the start, too, Jack Daniels was told to allow for right-hand-drive and left-hand-drive chassis. Whereas the TC had used a beam front axle allied to hard half-elliptic springs mounted close together, the Issigonis layout featured coil springs and wishbones, where hydraulic lever-arm

dampers also doubled as top wishbones in this linkage.

Compared with the TC, the TD had wider wheeltracks – 2.4in (60mm) at the front, and no less than 5in (127mm) at the rear. This increase, combined with tyres which placed more rubber on the road, meant that the TD should be a better-handling car than the TC had ever been – and so it proved in practice, too. Not only that, but there was the potential for much softer suspension, much more wheel movement than before, all allied to wider-rim/smaller-diameter road wheels. Issigonis, who was a great fan of rack-and-pinion steering, also made sure that such a system was specified for the TD.

This was the original TD rolling chassis, ready for final assembly. The chassis is clearly much more solid than the TC's had ever been.

The TA of 1936 reflected the classic, traditional, face of MG sports cars, complete with an upright grille, free-standing headlamps and a narrow wheel track.

MG's 'Octagon' badge, so simple, so distinctive, and unique, was recognizable all over the world. MG never needed to change it – and never have.

Larger, faster yet simpler than the PB which it replaced in 1936, the new TA was the first of the legendary T-series family.

When TB turned into TC in 1945, no visual style changes were needed. Look, indeed, at the original TA style and see if you can spot any differences.

The only way to pick out a TC – this car – from the earlier TA / TB types was that the cockpit was a bit wider and the cockpit surround pressings were altered slightly, to suit. The exposed spare wheel and the 'slab' fuel tank were typical of MG sports cars of the period.

The simple but unmistakable style of the post-war TC was nearly identical to that of the pre-war TA and TB types. T-Series cars like this were worshipped all over the world.

The TD of 1950 was the very first MG sports car to have independent front suspension and disc wheels. Compared with the TC, it was a squatter, more muscular-looking sports car.

Because of its disc wheels (wire-spokes were not available until after it was discontinued) the TD's style was always controversial.

Except for its engine and transmission, the TD was all-new for 1950, though its style was clearly developed from that of the TC.

The same, but very different: this was the TF of 1953 – 55, complete with a lowered nose, new-shape front wings and partly-recessed headlamps.

Sleeker, yet so simply different from the TD, the TF had a sloping bonnet, a sloping-back front grille, and was subtly modernized in many details.

The TF somehow looked smaller than the TD from almost every angle, yet the body centre section was just the same as before. The extra slope of the tank and the reprofiled rear wings had an influence from this angle.

Space, but only just, for the TF engine under the bonnet panels of this final T-Series car.

The 'TF1500' badge appeared on those cars built with the 1,466cc engine in 1954 and 1955 – this was actually the only time a 'T' badge appeared anywhere on the badging of this model family.

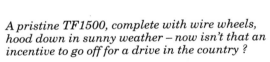

A pristine TF1500, complete with wire wheels, hood down in sunny weather – now isn't that an incentive to go off for a drive in the country?

Nowadays, of course, it would all be rejected as unaerodynamic, but in 1936, on the TA, wasn't this a neat way of combining a fold-flat screen with a rear view mirror?

'Cecil Kimber was always happy if he could get MG octagons on his cars' – even, like this, on a door handle.

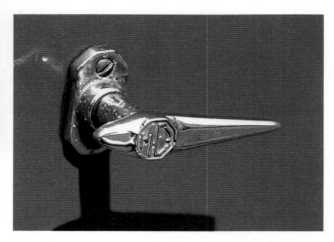

The TA's 1,292cc engine filled most of the available bonnet space, but everyday maintenance was still straightforward enough.

Not a line out of place, and not a surplus part – the neat and efficient front end of a late-1940s TC.

A place for everything and the speedometer ahead of the passenger's eyes, this being a TC facia panel of the late 1940s.

The TF of 1953 – 55 was fitted with a central instrument display with octagon-style surrounds.

On the TD – the first T-Series sports car to be available with right-hand or left-hand steering – the speedometer and rev-counter were always ahead of the the driver's eyes.

Because of the narrow confines of the bonnet, the TC's air cleaner had to be mounted above the tappet cover.

Not consciously styled, but beautifully detailed – the TA of 1936.

Detail of the rear of the TD's chassis shows that the side members were swept up and over the line of the rear axle; this was the first time a Midget had had this layout since the original M-Type.

I must stress what an innovation this was in 1938. Nowadays, of course, almost every new model uses a rack-and-pinion (often with hydraulic power assistance), but in 1938 it was almost totally unknown in the UK. Invented way back in the 1880s, rack-and-pinion had never been adopted for mass-production cars, because some engineers still thought it a rather crude mechanism. Issigonis, the deep thinker, knew better, got his way – and the rest is history.

Now we come to the vexed question of the road wheels. Up to and including the TC, every Abingdon-built MG sports car had been supplied with centre-lock wire-spoke wheels as standard, and even the Cowley-designed SA, VA and WA types had also used wire wheels. The problem, as far as Nuffield's accountants were concerned, was that wire wheels were costly, and always likely to go rattly and out-of-round in service. So for the Y-Type saloon – and

for the YT Tourer which evolved from it – bolt-on steel disc wheels were standardized, and there was no wire-wheel option, not even at an extra cost. When the time came to engineer the TD, therefore, Y-Type steel disc wheels were adopted, and no amount of nagging, pleading or table-banging from Abingdon could change all that.

The result, at first, was that the TD would look considerably less sporting than the TC. Even though the new wheel/tyre size was much squatter than before – 5.50-15in tyres on 4in-rim steel wheels, compared with 4.50-19in tyres on narrow-rim wire-spoke wheels – this did nothing for the new car's looks. Not even the addition of perforations to the wheels, early in the run, could make much difference. And Nuffield couldn't defend any of its actions, not even so far as to claim common ground with the Y-Type/YT models, which used 16in diameter wheels!

A lot of PR nonsense (today we would

97

Familiar? Actually this is the TD/TF-style front suspension as used in the MGA which took over in 1955.

Compared with the TC, the TD looked similar, though it was of course different in every line, panel and fitting. For a British Midget enthusiast, the bumpers were a real novelty.

call it 'spin-doctoring') went into justifying the disc wheels. *The Autocar*, for instance, swallowed the party line that the layout of the independent front suspension meant that a 'somewhat undesirable arrangement of wire spokes would be necessary' – but how, then, did wire wheels come to be optional on the TF of 1953, which had the same suspension? It was pathetic, really, because cost, and cost alone, was the reason.

Although MG had been granted a new chassis frame, neither the time nor the capital resources were available for new engines or transmission 'building blocks' to be designed. The TD therefore had to rely on updated TC engine and gearbox parts,

along with a new generation of hypoid bevel rear axle, a type which was already being used in the Morris Minor, and was also to be used in the next version of the Y-Type saloon, the YB. The Morris Minor also had a 4ft 2in (1,270mm) track.

The 1,250cc XPAG engine was still rated at 54bhp at 5,200rpm – the same as in the TC – though it looked visually different because it used a circular air filter/air-cleaner bowl for the carburettors, and for packaging purposes the oil-filter bowl was mounted horizontally.

Although the TC's cast-iron gearbox casing was retained, the intermediate ratios were slightly wider than before. This meant that bottom gear was lower, and

This was the rear view of the TD, complete with solid bumper, square number-plate holder, and the perforated-disc wheels which became standard during 1950.

although I have never seen this confirmed, I am sure this was done partly to counterbalance the use of smaller-diameter road wheels and therefore lower gearing. New for the TD was a different casing extension and low-line type of remote-control gearchange.

The hypoid bevel axle's ratio was 5.125:1, the same as that of the old-type axle of the TC, but as we have said, because of the TD's smaller wheels this meant that the new car would be significantly lower-geared than before. Taking 60mph (97km/h) as a comfortable cruising speed for this period, the TC's engine would have been turning over at 3,788rpm, but the TD would be revving at 4,167rpm: maybe not a lot more, but noticeable.

NEW STYLE, OLD THEME

While all this chassis work was going on, Jim O'Neill was developing a new body style for the TD at Cowley. Although influenced by what Abingdon's team wanted to see on the new car, he had to undertake all the drawing himself – and he had to do it with little guidance from above, because (to use his own words): 'Vic Oak used to go around all the Morris drawing boards, but he never even stopped to look at my drawing. I concluded that Morris Motors were just not interested in MG.'

O'Neill's brief, vague in the extreme, was that he should develop a new style which retained the themes – Italians, no doubt, would call this 'the emotion' – of the TC, but which was less angular than the TC, more squat, wider to take advantage of the new chassis, and of course to allow for the independent suspension and the new chassis frame. He also had to make provision for right-hand or left-hand drive, though this only involved providing for different

pedal and steering-column mounts, and shaping a facia/instrument panel which could be 'handed'. In fact it was an enjoyable task because he knew that he would get exemplary service from the Morris Bodies branch, who would be producing the shells in quantity for delivery to Abingdon, and he also knew that an ash-frame skeleton and simple steel pressings or foldings would be used.

Even though Nuffield's accountants would have liked it otherwise, I understand that no element of the TC shell could be carried over for use in the TD – so the fact that cars were produced so soon after design and development began, was something of a miracle. Even today it would not be possible to produce pressed-steel panels – particularly large ones such as the bulkhead pressing of the TD – in six months! In any case, MG were not interested in carry-over shapes because the TD chassis, much wider and with smaller, fatter wheels, needed an entirely different cover. The fact that the rear track was so much wider than before meant that the cockpit could also be widened, to give more space for the two passengers and their kit.

First on Jim O'Neill's full-size drawing board, then in a single prototype (as far as I know, there was only one such), the TD style took shape. In spite of the fact that Nuffield had already schemed up the 'Midget Major' mock-up, which had rounded lines, a full-width tub, and headlamps recessed into the wings, there was no trace of that car in the TD. In the end, Abingdon's influence was restricted to John Thornley asking for a part of the shell to be lowered slightly. However, it quite clearly came from the same family, the same breed, that Abingdon had always built: traditionally shaped in every way, the body used a steel-over-wood skeleton of construction, and had flowing wings, running boards, free-standing headlamps and a massive, exposed slab fuel tank to which the spare wheel was bolted on a frame. As far as British buyers were concerned there was one major (and obvious) visual change: sturdy, chrome-plated, full-width bumpers, with vertical overriders, were fitted at the front and rear.

Surprisingly, the extra width of the TD's chassis was not all reflected in the new bodyshell itself. One might have expected to have seen the 5in (127mm) wider rear track reflected in the cockpit width, especially as the line of the rear axle was under the rear stowage area, but this was not the case. So although by any previous MG standards the TD had a roomier shell than before, one really needed to wield a tape measure to prove it. Independent road tests showed that the TD measured 45in (114cm) across the width of the bench seat squab, which compared with 44in (112cm) for the TC; and total leg-room (seat squab to pedals) was up from 36.5in (92.7cm) to 39in (99cm). With the soft-top erect there was no more headroom than before, although simple adjustment could be made to allow the rake angle of the seat squab to be varied.

Although the lines of the TD never changed from 1950 to 1953, the plain steel disc wheels were only used on the earliest examples, soon being replaced by perforated disc types.

Even so, the final shape and style of the TD was seductive for its passengers, both in fine weather, when the soft-top could be furled back and the detachable side curtains stowed, and also at night, in cold weather, when the interior felt snug, the car made all the right noises, the long bonnet stretched ahead, and all felt right with the (sports-car) world. It was still, of course, sold without any form of heater (and none was listed, not even as an optional extra), and the wheel-close-to-chest driving position meant that the driver had to shuffle the rim between his hands in the best police-approved manner; but MG enthusiasts were all used to that, and did not complain.

The steering column was adjustable for length, and left-hand drive was at last available for export territories; and this, allied to the softer ride, the pin-sharp steering and the better (two-leading-shoe) brakes confirmed an all-round improvement.

Very little testing and development driving was possible before the design had to be 'frozen' for production, although one problem needed resolving immediately: right from the very first stage, the prototype exhibited the sort of scuttle shake which makes some cars memorable, and in the case of the TD it made the instruments impossible to read at speed, and the steering wheel felt very unpleasant. Charles Griffin, later to become a very senior engineer indeed at Longbridge (BMC and British Leyland), related how he found this to be quite intolerable. The chosen solution was for a large tubular brace to be added to the chassis frame, looping above the passengers' legs, out of sight behind the facia panel (the 'towel rail', as Griffin called it!), to which the bodyshell/scuttle was bolted at each corner; this was not completely successful, however, and the TD had to live with an element of shake throughout its career.

After what must have been a frantic race

Although the TC's basic style was carried forward for the TD, the bodyshell was completely new, being wider, squatter and subtly different in every way. For MG enthusiasts, the biggest shock was the standardization of steel disc wheels, which had never before been found on a Midget.

As expected by every previous MG buyer, the new TD had a similar style, along with useful features such as a fold-flat windscreen and cutaway doors.

to get production tooling ready, the very first TD – chassis no. TD0251 – was built at Abingdon on 10 November on an assembly line still full of the last TCs, with twenty-two further examples being assembled later in the month. Well before it was officially launched on 18 January 1950, the TD was in full series production, for at least 200 cars had already been built by that time, almost all of them filling the 'pipeline' across the Atlantic to North American buyers.

It is only when one looks back to magazine descriptions, such as the four-page article published in *The Autocar* on 20 January 1950, that the TD's importance becomes clear. Here, it seems, was a car which broke with so many old MG traditions, but which was still 'Safety Fast', and still so obviously from the same stable. *The Autocar* tried to get the name 'Midge' accepted by its readership, but failed completely. Even so, there was no mistaking technical editor Montague Tombs's feelings:

Everybody calls the well loved MG Midget the 'Midge', so it might just as well be printed. The Series TD may be new, but it still looks like a Midge, and has not 'gone all futuristic' – for which many thanks, people will say. A sports car ought to look like a sports car, and its innards ought to be accessible so that fans can personally keep it in tune; they should not be hidden beneath billows of bent tin.

One reason for the breathless reception was that the TD arrived at a very attractive price. In the UK, the last of the TCs had cost £528 (including all taxes), whereas the original TD was priced at £569. Such a modest price rise – £41 – looked bearable when the more advanced specification was considered.

In the USA, the TD also rang all the right sort of bells, principally because the British currency had only recently been devalued against the American dollar, which almost automatically meant that British goods were going to be cheaper in export markets. Thus, whereas in 1949 the TC had been priced at $2,395, in 1950 the

TD sold for $1,850: a much better car was therefore to sell for $545 less – which made the American-market TD a bargain by any standards.

All over the world MG dealers soon discovered that they could not get enough TDs to satisfy the demand. When *The Motor* tested FMO 265 in February 1950, Joe Lowrey and his colleagues recorded a top speed of 77.2mph (124.2km/h), with 0–60mph (0–97km/h) in 21.3 seconds, which made the car slightly (but significantly) faster than the TC had ever been:

Close on 900 miles ... leaves no doubt that as the MG Car Co. Ltd. progresses down the alphabet in type designations, so also it progresses upwards in the provision of those qualities which make the widest all-round appeal to motorists whose tastes lie in small open cars of above-average performance. This judgement is passed after ownership experience of two TA models, and more than passing acquaintance with the TB and TC types...

The TD and its Rivals in the UK

The TD went on sale in 1950, and by the end of that year, the roll-call of sports cars in this class looked this:

HRG (1,074cc)	£1,003.80
HRG (1,496cc)	£1,086.86
Jowett Jupiter (1,486cc) **	£1,086.86
MG TD (1,250cc)	**£569.36**
Morgan Plus 4 **	£652.84
Singer Nine Roadster (1,074cc)	£575.75

**The Jupiter and the Vanguard-engined Morgan Plus 4 were both introduced in September 1950.

Suddenly this was a more competitive class, though the smart new Jupiter was very expensive and, as usual, Morgan supplies were very limited. The HRG, however, was now looking archaic and was very costly, so its sales had almost dried up. Therefore by any measure, the TD was much the most successful sports car in this group.

From this side, the XPAG's engine installation looks similar to that of the TC, but note the different gearchange extension, and the different air-cleaner.

Compared to the TC engine/gearbox which it replaced, the TD used different manifolding and air-cleaners, plus a different gearchange extension. This is in fact a Mk II, with larger-size SU carburettors than the standard items.

(Lowrey was himself a fanatical HRG owner too, so he knew what he was writing about.)

The Motor, like *The Autocar*, noted that the new model was significantly heavier than the old – this was yet another reason that MG had juggled its gearing, in order to regain the acceleration needed – but it also noted that it clocked 77.2mph (124.2km/h) instead of the TC's 72.9mph (117.2km/h). Such a difference might be due to individual variation between engines, but perhaps it also meant that the TD was slightly – very slightly – less aerodynamically bluff than its predecessor; although: '...there is no doubt that, for high-speed cruising on a

105

typical Continental road, a higher axle would be welcome...'

As you might expect, the testers loved the new chassis:

From a comfort angle, the new chassis, with its wider track, i.f.s. and larger tyres, represents a very marked improvement. Gone entirely is the old sports-car harshness, the ride now giving a combination of firmness and freedom from road shocks which closely approximates to the ideal for a car of this type. This improvement is accompanied by a definite advance in general road-holding and cornering, particularly noticeable when a ridged surface is encountered unexpectedly on a fast corner.

There is some measure of oversteer and some slight trace also of roll ... Coupled with these qualities is a steering gear which is comparatively high geared, and effortless to use...

In all, the TD will prove to be a car which, like its forerunners, one takes to with enthusiasm and parts from with reluctance, the only difference being that both the enthusiasm and the reluctance are greater than before.

Later in the year Lowrey summarized his year's test-car motoring as follows:

Finally, the smallest of the 'performance' models, the MG Midget, was tested in its TD series form. This is a car which has aroused a storm of controversy among diehard sports car enthusiasts – as, in fact, did most of the MG models which later became universal favourites – and our verdict after experience of it was definite.

There may be justification for the comment that in 1950 a two-seater car can be made which weighs less than 2,000lb and is shaped to cause less disturbance of the air; the reply is that, at a [basic] price of

ú445, which is far below that of anything of equal merit, the 'TD' is a sturdy car offering much better comfort and roadworthiness than the preceding 'TC' model, accelerating well up to over 75mph, and despite the use of a low top-gear ratio, not being unduly fuel-thirsty. In fact, a definite step forward.

This summarized the TD's new-model appeal quite perfectly, for without doubt it was a much better car than any of its obvious rivals. With summaries like that, there is really no need to quote at length from those of *The Autocar* testers, except to see that they noted that the design had : 'gone ahead by a large stride...Overall, on journeys from point to point, the Midget has gained enormously for use in the hands of those who have no wish to endure any degree of suspension discomfort for the sake of their open-air motoring.'

A year later their summary of a year's test cars noted that:

...those who know their Midgets through the whole succession of series were mightily impressed by the improvement in riding comfort provided by the coil spring i.f.s., the light but very definite rack-and-pinion steering – both in principle as used on the $1\frac{1}{4}$-litre saloon already – and the convenience of the wider two-seater body.

A controversy broke out among enthusiasts on the subject – that subject again – of inevitably increased weight that went with added refinement, and also on the lower overall drive ratio as compared with the TC; but the very willing engine takes it happily, and the net result in most people's eyes is a considerable gain.

The TD came along at exactly the right time for MG. By 1950, production of British cars was already way above any pre-war

The XPAG engine as installed under the bonnet of the TD. Note how close the 12-volt battery is to the rear of the tappet cover (the battery got very hot in certain conditions), and also note the mechanical drive to the rev-counter from the tail of the dynamo.

level, and exports were surging ahead, helped along by the devaluation of sterling. In this, the TD's first year, British car production exceeded half a million for the very first time, nearly 400,000 of those cars going for export. Basically, the TD sent out all the right sort of messages to the clientele; it was almost as if MG had said something like: 'Yes, we know it was a time for a new model. We listened carefully to what you requested, but we still think you want a new Midget to look like a Midget. We didn't have a lot of money to spend on new facilities, but we think you're going to like this one.'

We did, of course. Reaction from the USA was ecstatic, and the planners at Abingdon were soon reshuffling their resources to build TDs as fast as possible. Even though seven different models – MGs and Rileys – were being built there in 1950, overall output was pushed up from 7,046 in 1949 to 10,430 in 1950, and would rise further in 1951, to 11,065. Although MG Y-Type assembly (1,827 cars in 1950) and Riley RM-Series production (3,588 in the same year) held up remarkably well, it was the surge of T-Series build which made the headlines. Only 2,911 TC/TD types had been built in 1949, but this soared to 4,767

This was an early stage of the assembly of the centre 'tub' of the TD bodyshell at the Morris Bodies branch in Coventry. The basic skeleton was wood, as were the floorboards and the panelling above the line of the rear axle.

This is a TD bodyshell centre section, as virtually completed at the Morris Bodies branch in Coventry, with a line of Riley RM-Series bodies behind it, which will shortly be transported to Abingdon. The TD was available in right-hand or left-hand drive, as can be seen by the matching holes in the bulkhead pressing.

The TD in the USA: Little Competition

When the TD went on sale in the USA in 1950 it replaced the TC, which was really in a tiny class. This, don't forget, was three years before the Triumph TR2 and the Austin-Healey 100 went on sale. According to the eminent American motoring historian, Richard Langworth: 'Even in 1952 the TD didn't have much competition. MG and Jaguar had the sports car market about 98 per cent to themselves...' Richard also provided the following table of 1952 USA retail prices, to make his point:

Crosley Hot Shot Roadster	$929
Singer Sports Roadster	$1,995
MG TD	**$2,115**
Jowett Jupiter	$2,850
Riley 2.5 Roadster	$3,340
Jaguar XK120 Roadster	$4,039
Nash-Healey	£4,063

As in the UK, therefore, the major sales competition came from the Singer Roadster and Jowett Jupiter models, both of which sold in tiny numbers. It was no wonder, therefore, that the MG TD sold so well in the United States once a stable dealer network had been established.

TDs in 1950, and would rise again to 7,451 in 1951.

Delivery statistics to the USA told their own story: 662 cars in 1949, 2,825 in 1950, and 5,757 in 1951. In mid-1950 monthly production of TDs for all markets neared 500, and within a year that had been pushed up to the 700 mark. British enthusiasts might not have liked to admit it, but this was where MG's future – and its profitability – lay in the next few years. Moreover it was soon clear that the Americans loved the new TD, not only because it had a much softer ride than the TC (which had been ultra-sporting, but which had needed a sort of motoring masochism to be enjoyed) but because it was more practical. In a country where bumpers were often used as the first line of attack in parking manoeuvres, the blades fitted to the TD were a blessing.

For the first two or three years of the 1950s, MG managers (led, from 1952, by John Thornley) were totally bound up with making more and more TDs. Selling the

cars was rarely an issue. On the other hand there was ample opportunity to improve the mechanical design, particularly as the original specification had been fixed in such a hurry.

Few changes were ever made to the body style and equipment – so it is difficult to identify an early-model TD from a late-model – and none at all to the basic tub/cockpit, seating and steel panels. Perforated road wheels (of which more later) were fitted to some cars from mid-1950, and to all before the end of 1950, while a different, circular type of stop/tail-lamp was specified from late 1952.

One change, the moving of the wind-screen-mounted wiper motor to the centre of the screen rail, was probably done for standardization purposes, but it also meant that a hard and craggy item was no longer ahead of the passenger's head. Good for safety, but still in an anachronous place: the wiper motor would not disappear from view until the TF came along in 1953.

109

ENTER THE 'TDII'

Over the years, most of the development effort went into improving the chassis and running gear. The pressed-steel road wheels, heavily criticized for their 'Plain Jane' looks when the car was introduced, were the first to be modified. MG reacted to the criticism, but they also took note of the comment made by early competition drivers, that brake cooling was poor so any extra circulation was welcome, and arranged for a series of perforation holes to be added around the hub caps. At the very end of the TD's production run, when a centre-lock wire-wheel kit had been developed for the TF, TD owners were told how they could update their cars. The Service Bulletin which details all the changes and new parts was numbered ACG 5163, and after the TD became obsolete some owners did update theirs – but I have never actually seen such a car.

The first important package of mechanical improvements came in the summer of 1951 (from engine number 9408) when a larger diameter clutch plate – 8in (20cm) instead of 7.5in (19cm) – was standardized, this necessitating a different flywheel and changes to the transmission casings, while the clutch withdrawal-fork shaft was enlarged from 0.6725in (17mm) to 0.75in (19mm).

From this juncture, chassis no. 9159, the cars are sometimes known as TDII (but not as Mark II – see below), engine numbers changing from XPAG/TD/9407 to XPAG/TD2/9408. You will search in vain for any identification on the outside of the car itself (for the TD never carried any badging on its tail); even at the time, in the autumn of 1951, magazines noted that the car was being carried forward, unchanged, into 1952.

Here's a novelty: a left-hand-drive Midget! The TD was the first-ever Midget to be available with the steering wheel on either side of the cockpit, and to accommodate this there was also a 'handed' type of instrument panel. On the TD, therefore, the speedometer and the rev-counter were always positioned in the driver's line of sight. Still no fuel contents gauge, however!

Later engine changes included a combined oil-filter body/oil-pump housing (from engine no. 14224), an enlarged sump pan (from engine no. 14948 – 10.5 pints/6 litres instead of 9 pints/5 litres) and a new camshaft profile (from engine no. 24116). Operation of the clutch was changed from cable to rod linkage from chassis no. 22251.

MK II

From mid-1950 until the end of the TD's production run, it was possible to buy what was advertised as a TD Mk II. Although there was no rigidly applied specification for these cars, all of them had slightly tuned-up engines, and a small number were intended purely for competition use. The Mk II story began in 1950, when the very first such car was allocated to Dick Jacobs as a race car (see Chapter 6), and the original team of 1950 'works' race cars were all based on the Mk II specification.

TD final assembly at Abingdon, in a process so flexible that other cars could also be accommodated, for that is an RM-Series Riley saloon well back in the line. Note that the assembly line is simplicity itself: the right-hand wheels roll between kerbs, to locate them, the left-hand wheels on a flat strip of concrete slabs. No re-jigging problem, therefore, to accommodate wider-track machinery!

Production Mk IIs had engines tuned to the level of special tuning stage 1/1A, which meant that they had between 57bhp and 61bhp, running on compression ratios of 8.6:1, with larger inlet and exhaust valves, stronger valve springs, H4 (1 1/2in) SU carburettors, and related details. The compression ratio was reduced to 8.1:1 from late 1952.

Some cars (but not all) had different engine distributors, some had Lucas sports ignition coils, and all had twin fuel pumps; this was allied to a raised (longer) final drive ratio (4.875:1 instead of 5.125:1) along with extra, adjustable, Andrex friction shock absorbers at front and rear.

Visual changes included chrome-plated (instead of painted) radiator slats, a black-and-white MG badge on the radiator, and (from late 1952) 'Mark II' badges on the bonnet sides and on the rear bumper.

For many years there was confusion as to how many of these cars were ever made, for the TD production records are not held by the BMIHT at Gaydon. The MG Car Club once claimed that only forty-seven true competition Mark IIs were ever made, whilst another analysis later claimed that in all, 1,022 Mk IIs had been made. A recent survey, most painstakingly carried out by BMIHT Archivist Anders Clausager, has produced the following definitive figures:

The total production of Mark IIs, therefore, was nearly 6 per cent of total TD assembly, and (as you might expect) a very high percentage of those cars went to North America. Note that exports to North America did not actually begin until early 1951, and peaked in 1952 when murmurs about the TD's rather limited performance were becoming general. To re-emphasize, not all Mk IIs had quite the same level of specification and equipment, and a few – a tiny percentage – had more highly tuned engines, aligned to one or other of the factory's 'Stage' kits. The very last Mark II was built on the very last day of TD production at Abingdon: 17 August 1953.

Road and Track compared the performance of a Mark II with a late-model TD in its issue of February 1953, noting that the standard car cost $2,157, whereas the Mark II cost $2,380 – $223 (or, at the existing rate of exchange £80). Their testers found that there was a noticeable, but not dramatic, improvement in performance. The Mark II's top speed was 81.25m/h/130.73km/h (a two-way average), which no T-Series car had ever before achieved, while 0–60mph (0–97km/h) was recorded in 16.5 seconds, significantly better than the TD, which clocked 19.4 seconds. *Road and Track* pointed out the difficulties in comparing the two cars, noting

Destination	1950	1951	1952	1953	Total
Home market	4	0	2	45	51
Export (RHD)	24	11	4	12	51
Export (LHD)	2	0	0	11	13
Export (North America)	0	459	977	157	1,593
Chassis only (LHD)	1	0	0	1	2
Total	31	470	983	226	1,710

the fact that the Mark II had the higher rear axle ratio, and that the TD was better run in for this occasion. They concluded:

> Remember, the MG is a genuine sports car, with a gearbox designed to be used. If you want maximum performance the TDC [Mark II: author] will give it, and will stand up under extremely hard usage. If you want better tractability, less gear shifting, and somewhat smoother running – better buy the stock TD model.

STAGE TUNING

By the early 1950s MG had developed a whole range of tuning kits for the XPAG engine, selling these in hundreds, if not in tens of thousands, to TC, TD and (later) TF owners. John Thornley, who later wrote so knowledgeably about them in *Maintaining the Breed*, lists these as follows:

Stage TF1: Basically as fitted to the TD Mark II, already described:
    61bhp at 5,000rpm.

Stage TF2: As Stage 1, but 9.3:1 compression ratio. Required at least 90 Octane fuel:
    64bhp at 5,500/6,000rpm.

Stage TF3: As Stage 2, but with a new camshaft which featured 35 degrees of overlap:
    66bhp at 5,800/6,300rpm.

Stage TF4A: As Stage 3, but with a special fabricated exhaust manifold, which liberated a further two to three bhp all through the range.

(Note that the 'stage' numbering, and the number of different steps available, changed over the years, those quoted above also applying to TF1250s. More, even more ambitious tune-up kits were available, which involved the use of Shorrock superchargers.)

MATURITY

Although the TD was a brisk little sports car with great character, in some ways it was not as fast as it felt! Even so, a combination of low gearing, the urgent engine character, the poor aerodynamics and the exhilaration of wind-in-the-hair motoring all blended to provide an attractive package. *The Autocar*'s sports editor, John A. Cooper, summarized this very well when he borrowed a Stage 2-modified car from the MG dealer, Jarvis of Wimbledon, to make a rapid dash from London to Scotland and back, in October 1951. It was a car with a 9.3:1 compression ratio and 4.55:1 final drive ratio. Driving towards the north of England:

> We attired ourselves in suitable Arctic-style clothing, as most of the pleasure of a run in an open car disappears if you are forced to have the hood up ... Long before we left the Metropolis behind, it was obvious to us both that this was no ordinary Midget; its acceleration in the lower gears was vivid, and the special supplementary hand ignition control proved valuable in controlling the tendency to detonate, which was noticeable in spite of a liberal proportion of Octol in the fuel ... mile after mile was covered at an easy cruising speed of an indicated 4,800–5,000rpm (which, allowing for a degree of instrumental optimism and other imponderables, represents something in the region of 80mph) ... we also got involved in a discussion on steering characteristics, as a result of which we went twice round one roundabout while I

Even before the TD was designed, the stylists at Cowley proposed to develop this 'Midget-Major' on the basis of the newly launched Morris Minor platform. It would have been available in coupe or Roadster form.

The Midget-Major proposal (coded DO926) lined up for viewing at Cowley in 1948, between an MG YT Tourer, and a Morris Minor saloon. Could it have been a success?

BMC: Merging Nuffield with Austin

Although Morris Motors and Austin had been bitter rivals for more than thirty years (with Morris usually holding UK market leadership), the two companies eventually merged in 1952: thus from March onwards, when the British Motor Corporation came into existence, the two marques found themselves under the same corporate umbrella.

Morris (or, more accurately, the Nuffield Organization) and Austin might have got together years earlier if it had not been for Lord Nuffield's stubborn refusal to cede control. Nor did it help that Austin's chairman was Len Lord, the powerful character who had parted company with Lord Nuffield in 1936, vowing revenge, and joining Austin in 1938. Lord approached Lord Nuffield in 1948, and again in 1950, but was twice rebuffed. Finally the two agreed to collaborate in November 1951. To quote author Graham Turner: 'Lord once remarked that they were like two Second Division teams trying to play in the First Division. Altogether there seemed a good deal of logic in a merger: the only trouble was that Nuffield and Lord had not been on speaking terms for a long time.'

At first Lord Nuffield was BMC's chairman, while Len Lord was its deputy chairman and managing director; but from December 1952 Nuffield finally stepped down, to allow Lord to become BMC's undisputed master. He had always acted like that, in any case!

As far as MG and John Thornley were concerned, this put them further down the pecking order than ever before. Until 1952, new MGs were being designed at Cowley, and Thornley had been able to discuss policy with Nuffield's Reg Hanks. After that, he had to learn to relate to Len Lord, and Longbridge.

Although the industrial logic of a merger was impeccable, and Austin soon became the dominant force, Len Lord allowed the internal sales and marketing battle between Austin and Nuffield to continue for some years. The dynamic Lord was chief executive, just as he had been at Morris in the 1930s and at Austin in the 1940s, but he also acted as BMC's top product planner, designer and stylist – all in the same self-opinionated package. Therefore when Thornley requested approval and investment funds for the EX175 project towards the end of 1952, he was obliged to take the prototype car to Longbridge, for Len Lord's personal inspection.

As we now know so well, he was too late. Lord had already invented the Austin-Healey marque, which was to be sold through the existing Austin network at home and abroad. For the next few years MG, with the ageing T-Series line, would have to soldier on through the Nuffield dealer network.

Mergers, they say, should result in cost savings, synergy and greater efficiency. At BMC, however, this didn't happen for many years.

proved that the MG did, in fact, possess a slight tendency to oversteer... throughout the 740 miles covered the MG never gave a sign of trouble, and behaved perfectly. In all fairness to the car it should be said that really, for a compression ratio as high as that employed in this instance, petrol-benzole is a necessity if the best is to be got out of the engine; but in spite of the absence of that valuable commodity, the performance was quite remarkable on a mixture of Pool and Octol.

The handling is good, being a great advance on previous models by virtue of the use of i.f.s. of relative softness, while the power extracted nowadays from the familiar Midget engines gets more and more surprising. In every way this trip was a great success.

All in all, the TD's popularity reached its peak in 1952, when no fewer than 10,838 cars were produced – this, incidentally, exceeding the total achieved for the TC in four complete years! In one phenomenal month – May 1952 – no fewer than 1,185 TDs were produced, which was an outright record for any T-Series car, never again to be beaten; though more than 1,000 cars were also produced in September, October, November and in December of the same year.

Momentous events outside Abingdon – outside the control of Abingdon, even – then had their effect. Not only did Austin merge with the Nuffield Organization in 1952, a cataclysmic event which brought Len Lord of Austin back into contact with MG, but the prototypes of two ambitious new sports cars, the Triumph TR2 and the Austin-Healey 100, both appeared. So, good though it was – great, arguably – the TD Midget would soon need change and improvement. John Thornley's team had already designed EX175, a totally different car, but it had been rejected by Len Lord, so a facelifted TD – the TF – had to be developed in its place.

For the TD, the end came on 17 August 1953, when chassis no. 29915 rolled off the assembly line. In a mere forty-five months, no fewer than 29,664 TDs had been built.

TD (1949 – 1953)

Numbers built
29,664
Production period: November 1949 – August 1953

Layout
Ladder-type separate steel chassis frame, with steel panelled body panels on a wooden bodyshell skeleton. Two-door, front engine/rear drive, sold as a two-seater open sports car.

Engine

Type	Nuffield, Type XPAG
Block material	Cast iron
Head material	Cast iron
Cylinders	4 in-line
Cooling	Water
Bore and stroke	66.5 x 90mm
Capacity	1,250cc
Main bearings	3
Valves	2 per cylinder, operated by in-line overhead valves, pushrods and rockers, with camshaft mounted in block, driven by chain from crankshaft
Compression ratio	7.25:1
Carburettors	2 SU
Max. power	54bhp @ 5,200rpm
Max. torque	64lb ft @ 2,600rpm

Transmission
Four-speed manual gearbox, with synchromesh on top, third and second gears.

Clutch	Single dry plate

Overall gearbox ratios

Top   5.125
3rd   7.098
2nd   10.609
1st   17.938
Reverse   17.938
Final drive   5.125:1 (hypoid bevel)

14.4mph (23.17km/h)/1,000rpm in top gear

Suspension and steering

Front   Independent, by coil springs, wishbones, and hydraulic
                 lever-arm dampers
Rear   Live (beam) axle, with half-elliptic leaf springs and Luvax
                 hydraulic lever-arm dampers
Steering   Rack-and-pinion
Tyres   5.50-15in cross-ply
Wheels   Steel disc, bolt-on fixing, with centre-lock wire spoke
                 as optional equipment towards the end of the run
Rim width   4.0in

Brakes

Type   Drum brakes at front, drums at rear, hydraulically operated
Size   9 x 1.5in front and rear drums

Dimensions (in/mm)

Track
  Front   47.4/1,204mm
  Rear   50/1,270mm
Wheelbase   94/2,388mm
Overall length   145/3,683mm
Overall width   56.6/1,438mm
Overall height
  (hood erect)   53/1,346mm
Unladen weight   1,930lb/875kg

UK retail price

At launch in 1950:   £569.36 (basic price £445)
From April 1951:   £732.61 (basic price £470)
From autumn 1952:   £825.95 (basic price £530)

USA retail price

In 1950 $1,850
In 1951 $1,975
In 1952 and 1953 $2,115
In 1954 (unsold cars) $2,145

The TD Mk II was produced to special order from 1951 to 1953 with a more powerful engine and higher overall gearing:

Engine

Compression ratio	8.0:1
Max. power	60bhp @ 5,500rpm

Transmission

Top	4.875
3rd	6.75
2nd	10.10
1st	17.08
Reverse	17.08
Final Drive	4.875:1 (hypoid bevel)

15.2mph (24.46km/h)/1,000rpm in top gear

UK retail price

In 1953	£829.87 (basic price £585)

USA retail price

In 1951	$2,210
In 1952 and 1953	$2,360

6 Record Breaking, Racing and Rallying: Brave Efforts

'Great engine – shame about the shape': this is one way of describing the motorsport potential of the T-Series cars. Yet it all depends on what you mean by motorsport: where the sport demanded sleek streamlining and high top speeds, then T-Series cars started at a disadvantage; but where manoeuvrability, handling and sheer rugged strength were concerned, the cars were always in with a chance.

Although it is easy to criticize the T-Series cars' aerodynamic qualities (I once heard them compared to that of a barn door...), you have to remember that almost all sports cars were still shaped like that in the 1930s, when the T-Series family was conceived. A look at cars in the British marketplace of 1936 shows the TA looking very similar to the HRG, the Morgan 4/4 or the Singer Le Mans of the period, and that situation persisted into the 1940s, too.

The records show that T-Series cars, and especially the TB-TF XPAG/XPEG engines, had a great record in motorsport for many years. For much of the time, officially at least, there was no separate 'Competitions Department' at Abingdon, but this did not mean that MG's sporting expertise had dried up. Resourceful characters such as Alec Hounslow, Reg Jackson and Syd Enever were still around, while Cecil Kimber (at first) and John Thornley were always willing to bend a few rules, provide a great deal of technical support and preparation expertise, and even foot the bills at times.

Earlier in the 1930s Abingdon had supported a serious motor-racing programme, its products becoming more and more specialized as its ambitions grew, while it also helped teams of cars to become competitive in reliability trials. From mid-1935, however, Nuffield's Len Lord abruptly closed down the 'works' racing programme, accusing Kimber of spending far too much money on the sport without gaining extra sales to prove his point. Even then, however, Len Lord was not adamantly opposed to all types of sport, especially not to those which demonstrated the worth of production-line models. Accordingly, from 1935 MG concentrated its support on a series of cars for use in reliability trials, and helped individualists such as 'Goldie' Gardner to take a series of sensational speed records in MG-engined specials.

'CRACKERS' AND 'MUSKETEERS': THE TRIALS CARS

In the 1930s the reliability or 'sporting' trial was a peculiarly British form of motoring torture for which MG sports cars were ideally suited. A trial was a straight contest between motor car and the elements, but the odds were heavily loaded against

The famous 'Cream Cracker' trials team, which had previously used PAs and PBs, re-equipped with TAs for 1937, these cars being driven by Maurice Toulmin, Ken Crawford and John Jones.

Godfrey Imhof's VA-engined TA BBL 81, the 'Cream Cracker' car first seen in 1938, mounted its spare wheels ahead of the radiator on some occasions. Clearly this did nothing to improve traction, but in Imhof's opinion it increased front-end grip for driving tests.
[Magna Press]

the cars, which operated outside their normal habitat. In Victorian and Edwardian times, before World War I, trials were no more than a challenge to the primitive road cars of the day to complete a lengthy course on public highways. By the 1920s, though, the latest cars were too good, and the roads too much improved, for this still to be difficult.

Events such as the Exeter, Land's End and Edinburgh trials then evolved, where distances were still great, but near-impossible hills had to be climbed along the way. Cars were closely observed by marshals (hence the phrase 'observed sections'), and had to be kept moving at all costs. Next, shorter and tougher regional events developed – for example the 'Colmore' and the 'Gloucester' – these offering shorter link routes but a greater number of steeper and even more atrocious hills to be climbed. By the 1930s, almost every trials hill was on private ground, for their condition was usually too awful for regular public use. To be worthy of its name, each one had to be very steep, narrow, fierce, muddy, rocky, appallingly maintained, preferably twisty or with hairpin corners, and sometimes frankly too dangerous for ordinary cars to tackle.

As the sections worsened, the cars became more capable, so by 1938 when MG's quasi-'works' cars were at their peak, these were extremely specialized pieces of machinery. Although every Midget was the right basic sort of car for this esoteric sport, to be a truly successful trials car, weight (and equipment!) had to be removed

BJB 412 was the very last of the 'works' TA trials cars, a 1938/9 'Musketeer' powered by a supercharged 1,292cc engine, and driven by Dickie Green. [Magna Press]

Jack Bastock drove BBL 83, a 1938/1939 'Three Musketeers' TA, in 1938 and 1939.

wherever possible, and it needed to have even better traction, a tighter-than-standard steering lock, and an engine re-tuned to give as much low-speed torque as possible; the Midgets which had supercharged engines were particularly prepared with these criteria in mind.

Although MG had certainly helped individual trials drivers in earlier years, they had not backed any teams, nor was there any overt effort to produce a 'works-supported' atmosphere. From 1934 to 1939, though, MG supported three semi-professional trials teams of Midgets: the 'Cream Crackers' and the 'Three Musketeers' in England, and the 'Highlanders' in Scotland. No one really knows where the quirky team names came from – it was just

one of the habits of the 1930s that this sort of thing should be done! In all cases the drivers had already made their mark while driving their own cars, and although they were certainly not paid large retainers to ensure their loyalty to MG, the factory made it clear that they were expected to compete in no other make of car while contracted to an MG trials team; some of this group of 'works' drivers swopped from one team to another during the period.

The first 'Cream Cracker' team appeared in 1934 and 1935, these cars being much-modified PA Midgets, which were replaced by PB Midgets for 1935/1936; they were maintained at Abingdon, the PBs were supercharged, and every team member did fourteen or fifteen events during the season.

The original 'Musketeer' team had a hectic beginning. The first cars appeared in 1935 and were modified NE Magnettes, but from midsummer these were replaced by a set of PA Midgets which had already competed at Le Mans with lady drivers! Almost immediately those PAs were displaced by three very special Magnette/Magna specials, these evidently using parts from all manner of existing or older MG models – which proved just how much one model always depended on another for its development!

Both teams were then supplied with TA Midgets for 1937, though their specifications differed. By this time all the cars had locked (not limited-slip) differentials, they could run on 19in or 16in wire-spoke wheels, they always used 'knobbly' tyres,

and all competed in a huge number of events during the season. As every car carried an Abingdon-based registration number, there was no question of hiding their provenance. For 1937, the 'Cream Cracker' TAs (finished in a paint scheme of distinctive cream with brown wings) were registered ABL 960, 962 and 964, and were driven by Maurice 'the Colonel' Toulmin, Ken Crawford and 'Jesus' Jones. The 'Musketeer' TAs (with a red paint scheme) were ABL 961, 963 and 965 – very adjacent and very confusing – and were driven by R. A. Macdermid, Jack Bastock and Archie Langley.

As prepared at the factory, there was a very long list of modifications and improvements to these TAs, covering anything from aluminium in place of steel panels, twin

In 1937 the works-supported 'Cream Cracker' team used these three TAs, their drivers being (left to right) Maurice Toulmin, Ken Crawford and Johnny 'Jesus' Jones. Like the similar, but rival, 'Three Musketeers', theses cars might have looked standard, but in fact were heavily modified, with tuned-up engines, different gearboxes, lightweight body panels and locked differentials.

This was Maurice 'Colonel' Toulmin's 'Cream Cracker' TA tackling Ditch Lane in the Mid-Surrey AC's Experts' trial in 1938. These particular cars had 1.7-litre engines, and were built to withstand ferocious conditions. Make no mistake –this is an extremely slippery and very steep hill, the TA needing all its traction (helped by the knobbly tyres and the locked differential) to keep going.

spare wheels carried at the rear, high-compression engines, special gear ratios and the well proven locked differential, different wheels, dampers and road springs, and much protection of the chassis, engine and underside from damage on rough tracks. The transmission of all trials cars had a hard time, so it was quite usual for each team to carry at least one complete replacement differential as a spare, in case an installed diff. was disabled by serious torque reversals.

These cars were so successful that there were mutterings from rivals about 'works'

assistance; however, these can largely be written off as jealousy, because most of the modifications were also available (for money!) to a private owner. In any case, MG were enjoying their limelight, and produced two more TA teams for 1938. The 'Cream Cracker' TAs were BBL 78, 79, 80 and 81, and they had the same drivers plus a new recruit, London electrical retailer Godfrey Imhof, who would go on to win the RAC Rally in 1952. These were even more specialized than the original set of TAs, because in the search for torque they were originally fitted with tuned-up 1,548cc

There were limits even to what Abingdon could achieve with the 'works' TA trials cars – Johnny 'Jesus' Jones would have liked more lock to get him round this hairpin. Note the traction being developed through the rear tyres, even on this awful surface.

(VA-style) engines. Later in 1938 these engines were upgraded further to a unique 1,708cc, by using the 73mm bore pistons normally only found in the six-cylinder MG WA engines. The 'Cream Cracker' team was disbanded at the end of that season.

The 1938 'Musketeer' TA cars (which would also be used in 1939) were registered BBL 82, 83 and 84 along with BJB 412, and the 1937 team of drivers were joined by Dickie Green. The new 'Musketeer' team cars were very different from the 'Cracker' types, for they had 1,292cc engines fitted with Laystall crankshafts, and were supercharged by Marshall units. The 'blower', of course, had the effect of enlarging the engine's capacity, so the comparison between the two teams was still close.

In Scotland, the 'Highlander' team tended to take over one-year-old (but refurbished) cars from the English-based 'works' teams, repainting them Scottish blue and making further modifications. Keith Elliott, Norman Gibson and George Murray Frame (the latter also drove 'works' Sunbeam-Talbot rally cars in the 1940s and 1950s) were regular drivers.

Abingdon's support for sporting trials wound down rapidly in 1939, not because they had become bored with that sport, but because the whole sport of trials was in crisis. Even in those days, when traffic densities were a mere 10 per cent of what they are today, there were growing public complaints of congestion caused by spectators, public nuisance, high speeds in all the

Archie Langley trickling through the ford at the base of the famous trials hill at Kineton, in Warwickshire, in one of the 1938 'Three Musketeers' MG TA, which were equipped with supercharged engines. Like BBL 82 and BBL 83, this was a specially developed competition car from Abingdon, with shielded underside, special suspension, engine and transmission.

Pat Moss (left) and Pat Faichney drove the TF1500, KRX 90, in minor British events, then in the RAC International rally of 1955. [Magna Press]

wrong places, and the dropping of mud on public highways. [To those of us who loved road rallies in the 1960s, a sport which was also hounded slowly to extinction by public opinion, this all sounds very familiar !]

A surprising number of these 'works' trials cars have survived, and some are still used in the modern production-car equivalent of the events they tackled in their heyday.

LE MANS RACING: A LOST CAUSE

Although the Le Mans Twenty-Four Hour race was all about endurance, super-streamlined bodies and high top speeds, one enthusiastic private owner, George Phillips, raced there with T-based special cars on three occasions: 1949 to 1951. Although he only ever managed to finish the French classic once, his cheerful optimism impressed everyone.

Phillips was an extrovert ex-RAF character who seemed to enjoy every moment of his leisure time (which explains why he later joined Gregor Grant at *Autosport* as chief photographer, a somewhat chaotic magazine in its early days, where a sense of humour was also needed...) and went racing for fun. According to John Thornley he was 'bluff, genial, endowed with almost unlimited powers of invective and an entirely synthetic bad temper'. He knew he could not win Le Mans in an MG, nor probably the capacity class either, but he was determined to have a great deal of fun in trying.

For the 1949 Le Mans race, Philips decided to modify a TC which he had earlier bought for British motor racing. Recognizing straightaway that the standard body style would not be satisfactory, he discarded the standard shell completely,

substituting an ultra-light, low-slung, open two-seater shell, one which featured headlamps built into each side of the grille, and with cycle-type front wings. Experience now suggests that the aerodynamic performance of the new shell was still not good enough to make it class-competitive, but by 1949 standards it certainly looked, handled, and sounded like a racing car.

Before the race neither of the 'establishment' magazines (*The Autocar* and *Motor*) even mentioned that the TC had been entered. Phillips, who didn't care about such things, took 'Curly' Dryden along as his co-driver, and the two just kept plugging away for nineteen exhausting hours. At one stage an explosion in the silencer of the car, just as he started to refuel at the pits, caused a fire – so Phillips drove the car out of the flames; then in the nineteenth hour it halted out on the circuit with an electrical failure. After which, to quote *The Autocar*: 'The MG had been flagged off because a mechanic went to attend the car on the course, tried to advise the driver on how to change a [distributor] condenser, and then was persuaded to come in the car to the pits!'

Phillips repeated the entry for 1950, using the same rather stark-looking car, but further developed with engine preparation help from MG at Abingdon. Partnered this time by gentleman-racer Eric Winterbottom, Phillips and the TC made no mistake, finishing 18th overall in the 1.5-litre class, immediately behind the 'works' Jowett Jupiter which won that section of the event. Averaging 73mph (117.5km/h) for the twenty-four hours – this being the same figure as the top speed of a production-type TC – this was a splendid performance and one which told us a lot about the rugged reliability of TC-Series running gear. MG, in fact, were so impressed by this performance that for

Autosport *photographer George Phillips drove this special-bodied TC in the Le Mans Twenty-Four Hour sports-car race of 1949 and 1950.* [Magna Press]

Those were the days –1949 –when you could still park a Le Mans race car in a London street without causing a traffic jam or attracting the attention of a warden. This was George Phillips' special-bodied TC, as privately prepared for use in the Le Mans Twenty-Four Hour Race.

1951 they agreed to build a special-bodied TD for Phillips to race at Le Mans. This car, and the evolution which led to it becoming the ancestor of the MGA, is described in Appendix 3.

TC AND TD IN RACING

MG, and Cecil Kimber in particular, were deeply upset when Len Lord ordered the closure of the already-famous competitions department in 1935. There were to be no more specialized models such as the Q-Type and R-Type Midgets, and no more cars with supercharged engines. Although they could, and did, help heros like 'Goldie' Gardner and Captain George Eyston (see below) with their MG-badged record cars, MG would no longer have production cars which were suitable for motor racing. In the 1930s, therefore, MG concentrated on developing the 'works' trials cars which have already been described, and it was not

until after the war when the TC had gone on sale, that thought was given to any other approach. However, the TC was never truly competitive, even in the parochial world of British club racing, although the XPAG engine was much admired, and used in all manner of specials.

Britain's first-ever production car race was held at Silverstone in August 1949, and was the sort of showcase event which begged for an MG presence; so John Thornley made sure that three 'privately prepared' TCs – though there was in fact a lot of factory involvement in these machines – took part, driven by Dick Jacobs (an MG dealer), George Phillips and Ted Lund. Faced as they were by a team of 1 1/2-litre HRGs, this was never likely to be an easy contest, and in a race quite dominated by three of the new Jaguar XK120s, the MGs and the HRGs had to fight their own, low-profile battle. Dick Jacobs kept up with Eric Thompson's class-leading HRG

'Works' TDs were raced in British Production Sports Car events in the early 1950s, but were always handicapped by being in the 1.5-litre category and therefore up against cars like the HRG which leads Ted Lund and Dick Jacobs here, at Silverstone in August 1950.

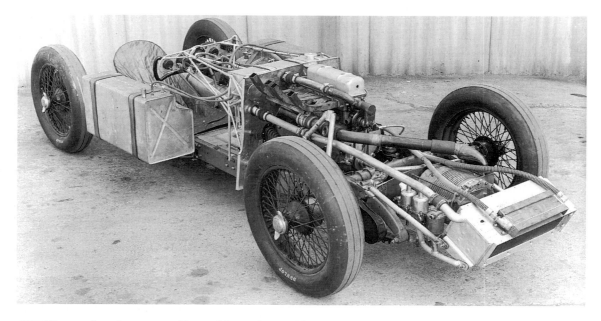

EX135 was already a venerable, and legendary, MG record car by the time it was re-engined yet again in 1951, this time with a supercharged version of the XPAG engine. The huge 'blower' is installed up front, between the chassis members, while the exhaust stubs point out through tiny holes in the streamlined bodyskin.

This rear view of EX135 shows how the XPAG engine fitted very neatly into its overall body profile. Note the off-set drive line, which allowed the driver's seat to be lowered by several inches and moved inboard.

for much of the hour-long race, but after going off the road at one point, he dropped back.

Although all three TCs made it to the end of the race – in the order Lund-Jacobs-Phillips – they were headed in the 1 $^1/_2$-litre class by three HRGs and Peter Morgan's 1.26-litre engined Morgan. Even so, it was extremely close, because the leading HRG averaged 71.04mph (114.3km/h), and the fastest TC, 68.93mph (110.9km/h) – which, if nothing else, reflected the fact that the HRGs had considerably larger engines.

In the following year Jacobs and Phillips were both able to take an early look at the TD, testing it with a view to going racing, and discovering – as if it was not going to be obvious – that the drum brakes would have a very hard time behind the plain steel disc wheels: it was not long after this that the perforated discs were adopted. Dick Jacobs used FMO 885, which was effectively the prototype TD Mk II, to beat the 1$^1/_2$-litre HRGs at Blandford, and later three new 'works' TDs – FRX 941, 942 and 943 – were prepared for the Silverstone Production Car race, and later for the Tourist Trophy race. Silverstone was in August, and the TDs competed in a race limited to 2-litre cars; this time the MGs were more competitive, for Dick Jacobs's machine finished second in its class to Ruddock's HRG, averaging 71.27mph (114.7km/h), with Ted Lund's and George Phillips' cars close behind him.

For the Tourist Trophy, revived for the first time since 1938, the TDs ran in full Mk II tune, which allowed them to have the increased compression ratio and, importantly, the larger carburettors of those cars. The TT was held on the new Dundrod circuit in Northern Ireland, this being a triangle of more than 7.4 miles (11.9km) of narrow public roads which had been closed

specifically for the occasion. For MG there was good news and bad news, the good news being that as a three-hour event it would allow their reliability to count, the bad news being not only that the weather was consistently awful, but that the fastest cars (Jaguar XK120s) were set to lap the TDs every six or seven minutes throughout the day! Thirty-one cars started, all struggled with the conditions, and every car must have spun, threatened to spin, or overshot corners at least once during the day. Although Tommy Wisdom's 1$^1/_2$-litre Jowett Jupiter led the class at first, he soon broke the Jowett's troublesome flat-four engine, and it wasn't long before the 'works' TDs were in complete command of this category.

At the end of three hours, to quote *The Autocar*: 'The TD MGs scored a resounding 1-2-3 success among the 1$^1/_2$s, although Lund (who had taken over the class lead when Dick Jacobs spun round) toured in slowly, having run a big end in the last two laps...'

Although average speeds were meaningless in these monsoon conditions, it is enough to say that Jacobs' class-winning TD averaged 63.29mph (101.83km/h) for three hours and so also finished 16th overall, and that no car with an engine smaller than 2-litre finished ahead of them. The lessons, though, were all around: first and foremost, the TD's 1.25-litre engine placed them at a disadvantage in that it put them in a capacity class which was invariably 1 $^1/_2$-litres, where larger-engined cars such as the latest Jowett Jupiter were likely to appear. The team of 1950 TDs, therefore, were farmed out to their drivers; the financial arrangements were not publicized, but MG insisted that preparation was always carried out away from Abingdon.

The cars were, in fact, already at the limit of their development (unless any of

The new MG EX179 record car was built up in 1954, on the basis of a much-lightened prototype MGA chassis frame, and was fitted with a tuned-up version of the latest XPEG 1,466cc engine. It set new speeds at Utah, in the USA, at almost the same time as the XPEG-engined TF was going into showrooms in the same Continent.

the homologation rules were to be broken, which was something a reputable company like MG would not consider). Undoubtedly the highspot of the season was that Dick Jacobs once again competed in the *Daily Express* Production Car race at Silverstone, not only winning the 1 1/2-litre class of this one-hour event at 72.66mph (116.9km/h), but setting a fastest lap of 75.36mph (120.67km/h). Once again it was a 'works' Jowett Jupiter which led the class, but once again its engine blew up – and all three of the fancied HRGs were behind him this time. This was very satisfying for MG, who decided that it was an appropriate time to bring down the curtain. They were right, because at the TT a phalanx of Jupiters finally proved that car to be reliable, while George Phillips's TD retired with a broken clutch.

RALLYING

In Europe, and even more so in Britain after the war, it took a very long while for long-distance rallying to creep back onto the agenda, and MG took no interest until the 1950s. As in motor racing, the 1.25-litre engine size of the TDs was always a handicap, especially in the mountains where there was really no substitute for deep-breathing power units. Since open two-seater TDs were not suitable for high-profile events like the Monte, they only really shone in events demanding manoeuvrability, and skills in driving tests. A foreign team of private owners won a team prize in the 1950 French Alpine (one of the cars also winning the 1 1/2-litre class), but in 1951 the hated rivals from HRG got in the way, and there were no major successes in the RAC rally, which was revived from 1951.

If BMC had not elected to re-open a competitions department at Abingdon, to be managed by Marcus Chambers, the T-Series rallying story might have ended there. However, in 1955 Chambers started by trying almost every car in the BMC range in a whole variety of events. Thus for the RAC rally in March his mechanics prepared seven cars: three Austin Westminsters, three MG ZA Magnette saloons, and a lone TF1500 for an unknown girl call Pat Moss – unknown, that is, in rallying terms, for she was Stirling Moss's sister, she was already making a name for herself in the sport of horse jumping, and she had also already tackled a rally or two in her own Triumph TR2.

Invited to use the TF1500 in the RAC rally, an event she had never before done or even seen, Pat took Ms Pat Faichney with her as co-driver, and learned the ropes of rallying as she went on! It would be gratifying to be able to report a fairytale result, but there was none: the weather was wintry to say the least, some driving tests, sections and circuits had to be cancelled, and it needed real experience even to reach the finish.

For the TF1500 it was something of a swansong, but for Pat it was a solid beginning, as she finished third in the Ladies' class. Within a year or so she would always be a top contender for the ladies' category, and by the end of the 1950s she would be shooting for outright victory.

RECORD CARS

MG's interest in the development of specialized record cars began in 1930 with Capt George Eyston's EX120, and not even Len Lord's disapproval of motorsport in all its forms could wean the company away from this branch of the sport. EX127 followed in 1931, and one of the most famous of all MG record cars, EX135, was built in 1934. Beautifully streamlined, and originally having a K3 Magnette chassis and off-set transmission, this car had an extraordinary career, because in much modified and greatly developed form it was still breaking records nearly twenty years after its original construction as an open-wheeled car for use at Brooklands and elsewhere. First used by George Eyston in 1934, it was repurchased by MG in 1937, rebodied with a sleek, full-width style drawn up by Reid Railton of Thomson & Taylor, and loaned out to Major 'Goldie' Gardner. To keep Nuffield's policies intact, it was henceforth to be known as the Gardner-MG, and treated as his own property. Gardner later bought the car.

It was first fitted with supercharged ohc engines, then (in 1948) with a four-cylinder prototype Jaguar 'XK100' unit; later it was given a much-modified six-cylinder Wolseley unit, and finally, in 1951, was fitted with supercharged XPAG engines. Reg Jackson and Syd Enever were both involved in the re-engineering of this by now venerable old car, there being a choice of XPAG engines: one in highly tuned 'sprint' form (which meant that it did not have to last long before wilting under high boost pressures!), the other being a more durable 'endurance' unit.

The 'sprint' 1,250cc engine had a compression ratio of 9.3:1 which, along with 30lb (13.5kg) of boost and the use of methanol fuel, resulted in no less than 213bhp at 7,000rpm. Quite remarkable, indecently so, in fact, for an engine that had started life in 1938 at 1,140cc and with 39bhp !

The 'one-hour', or 'endurance' engine had a 7.25:1 compression ratio, and a mere

EX179 was as slippery as a fish, its XPEG engine totally hidden away, except for the (blanked off, for shipment) row of exhaust stubs which protruded through the light-alloy skin.

10lb (4.5kg) of supercharging, this resulting in 'only' 92bhp at 5,400rpm. To quote John Thornley from *Maintaining the Breed*: 'For 1951, therefore, the plot emerged to endeavour to show that the current [XPAG...] engine, with pushrods, and designed originally for ordinary passenger car motoring, was as strong and as good as its O.H.C. predecessor which had been designed originally for supercharging. The venue would be the Bonneville Salt Flats in Utah, USA, and the target would be 210mph [338km/h].'

Thornley also noted that to make such an expensive trip just for brief straight-line runs didn't make much economic sense, so: 'The answer was to take alternative engines and axles, and assail the 1-hour record which stood to the credit of Bugatti at 119.01mph [191.49km/h], together with the distance records, 50km, 50 miles, etc, which would be collected on the way.'

In 1951 the endurance running on a 10-mile (16km) circular track was highly successful, with Gardner taking six new International Class F (1½-litre category) records at up to one hour, when the mark was no less than 137.4mph (221.07km/h) – which tells us a lot about the streamlining efficiency of the bodyshell which had been

Under the skin of George Phillips' 1951 Le Mans contender was a TD Mk II rolling chassis. Compared with the TD road car, this special machine looked deliciously sleek and purposeful. Note the complete absence of a near-side door, for this was not required by Le Mans

For 1951, MG developed a special-bodied version of the TD for George Phillips to drive at Le Mans. This style was clearly much more aerodynamically efficient than the production-line TDs, and produced a much higher top speed. In basic shape, if not in detail, it also inspired the birth of the MGA in 1955.

designed in 1937. At the same time, the Gardner-MG also took ten American Class records, one hour (from a flying start) of racing being completed at 139.3mph (224.13km/h).

Although the highly tuned XPAG engine was not at fault, the 'sprint' section of the attempt was not a success, firstly because of persistent breakages in the timing equipment (supplied, mandatorily, by the American authorities), and later because storms waterlogged the salt desert on which the 14-mile (22.5km) straight track was laid.

For 1952, Gardner and EX135 made a further, determined attempt at Utah – but the expedition was complicated by the decision to take along a much-modified overhead-camshaft six-cylinder Wolseley engine (249bhp/2-litre) to fit to the car in order to tackle Class E records, too. By the time the Wolseley-engined attempts had been made, the car had been involved in a high-speed crash in which it had spun at more than 150mph (240km/h) and hit one of the marker posts defining the circular track, this then smashing the perspex canopy over the driver's helmet, hitting him quite hard. Gardner, though dazed, shrugged it off, and it was only later obvious that the blow to his head had been more serious than he ever admitted. In the meantime, EX135 was patched up, and the XPAG 'sprint' engine was fitted in place of the troublesome Wolseley unit.

Before MG's lease of the Bonneville area ran out, there was only time for limited running with the XPAG engines, when it became clear that the car was rather undergeared. New International Class F records were achieved for the Flying 5 Miles (at 189.5mph/304.9km/h) and the Flying 10 Km (182.8mph/294.1km/h). For the next day the rear axle ratio was changed from 2.9:1 to 2.8:1, and the car

went out again, recording a best of 202.20mph (325.34km/h) for the Flying 5 Km. Although these figures were good enough to break more American national figures, they still fell short – just short – of those set by EX135 on the German tarmac in 1939.

Further plans were laid for 1953, this time for EX135 to run on the Jabbeke road in Belgium and with a 231bhp /1,517cc XPEG-type engine; but Gardner was by now very ill and the expedition was cancelled. Some time later, MG bought EX135 back, after which it was converted into show-car status with various perspex display panels let into the light-alloy bodywork. It is now in the British Motor Heritage collection at Gaydon, still with one of the supercharged XPAG engines installed.

In the meantime George Eyston, the original owner of EX135 in 1934, had visited BMC's chairman, Len Lord, had waved considerable Castrol sponsorship, and asked if he could drive EX135 again at Utah. This plan foundered because the car was still owned by Gardner, and had always carried Duckham's sponsorship (a rival oil company!). However, Lord approved the building of a replacement car, so MG was allowed to design and build a new model, EX179: built up around the spare EX175 chassis frame (see Appendix 3), it might have looked like EX135, but it was mechanically novel and completely different in detail.

Many years afterwards Terry Mitchell, who designed that body, was quoted as saying: 'Syd Enever said to me that he wanted the new car to look like EX135, but be different – a typical Syd remark!'. For Mitchell, influenced by what Eyston was learning from his friends in the aerospace industry, this cannot have been easy, for the EX175 chassis had a shorter wheelbase

By the time George Phillips had added two leather straps to hold down the bonnet, and a couple of extra driving lights to improve night-time vision, the special-bodied Le Mans TD car was not quite as smooth as it might have been. This action study shows that the layout of the TD frame meant that Phillips had to sit up quite high, protected only by a small aero screen from the 100mph (160km/h)-plus blast of flat-out motoring on the Mulsanne straight.

This was the facia style of George Phillips' 1951 TD-based le Mans car: complete with octagonal-style instruments, which were not then in production.

than that of EX135, it also had independent front suspension, and there was more vertical wheel movement all round. Even so, this was a remarkably slippery body, for tests showed that it would only need 51bhp on the Utah Salt Flats for EX179 to reach 125mph (200km/h).

Powered originally by a specially prepared, normally aspirated XPEG (TF1500) type of engine, but later to have various other engines installed – both smaller and larger varieties – it was ready for use at Utah in 1954. Happily for MG's marketing efforts, the TF1500 had gone into production just before the runs were made, so the American MG dealers could relate any success gained by EX179 to the latest Abingdon sports car model.

As in 1951 and 1952, two versions of the XPEG engine were prepared: a 'sprint' unit with 97.5bhp at 6,500rpm, and an 'endurance' unit with 84bhp at 6,500rpm, the major difference, of course, being that neither unit was supercharged. Running on methanol, the 'sprint' unit used two extremely large SU carburettors, an 11.8:1 compression ratio and wild camshaft timing; the '12-hour' engine ran on 1 3/4in SUs and a 10.7:1 compression ratio. On both units the exhaust manifolds were, literally, four short, rectangular-section pipes linking the cylinder head to a row of outlets in the bonnet of the car, to the right of the body centre-line – all of which explains why the original EX179 was a left-hand-drive car!

In August 1954 EX179 started its runs at Utah with the '12-Hour' engine installed. George Eyston and the American driver Ken Miles shared the work, carrying out back-to-back three-hour shifts around the 10-mile (16km) circle before making a hurried stop to change drivers and to refuel. Soon after breakfast, and seemingly without strain, EX179 settled down to lap at around 124mph (200km/h) – meaning that it took nearly five minutes to complete one vast lap. Twelve hours later it had set seven new International Class F and 25 American national records, all at or close to 120mph (193km/h).

The following day the 'sprint' engine was installed, the axle ratio was changed, and (after a cable to Abingdon had confirmed this) Ken Miles was installed as the driver. Once again running on the 10-mile circle, EX179 achieved a lap in 153.69mph (247.29km/h), which was quite sensational for an unsupercharged 1.5-litre engined car!

Thus compared with 1952, when almost everything had seemed to go wrong, EX179's debut had been a totally reliable triumph, so the Abingdon team returned home well pleased. However, although EX179 still had a great career ahead of it – it was last used, much changed, as EX219 in 1959 – this was the last-ever record run by T-Series-engined cars. Indeed, by this time the engine and the cars it powered were due for retirement, as the TF, as I shall describe in the next chapter, was only a short-lived model.

7 TF: The Final Fling

If the last of the T-Series line, the TF, had sold better than it did, any number of Abingdon personalities might have claimed credit. As it turned out, it was no more than a short final fling, a pretty, facelifted version of the TD, much more appreciated in later years than it was when it was on the market in the 1950s. Moreover, if Jack Tatlow, MG's general manager, and John Thornley had got their way in 1952, the TF would never have been built, not even a single car. Along with chief engineer Syd Enever, that was the year in which they first proposed to replace the TD with a sleek new car, coded EX175. Basing its style on that of the one-off TD-based Le Mans car of 1951, and using modified TD running gear in a sturdy new chassis, he offered this to his new boss at BMC for approval – and was rebuffed!

The story of the EX175's arrival is described in detail in Appendix 3, one significant point being that the car was designed in the first few months of BMC's existence. Unhappily for MG, this was exactly the wrong time to suggest the right car, as Thornley later confirmed: 'We showed the car to Len Lord [BMC's chief executive] to get permission to produce it, but three days before he'd had Donald Healey up with the Healey 100, and as far as he was concerned, they were no different – so he certainly wasn't going to have this MG thing, because he'd got the Healey...'

During Gerald Palmer's tenure as chief designer at Cowley, he once proposed to replace the TD model with a new type of MG sports car, which could have had several different styles on a single basis. This version would have looked like a thoroughly up-dated T-Series theme, and might have appealed to the traditionalists. [David Knowles]

BMC and Austin-Healey

Geoffrey Healey always denied that there had been any kind of 'design competition' in 1952 when Len Lord chose to back the original Healey 100 in place of MG's EX175 project. Perhaps it was pure spite which led Lord to dismiss the EX175 project at this time – but there was no doubt that he was facing sports car submissions from all sides. Officially or unofficially, he encouraged several entrepreneurs to think of ways of designing sports cars around the 2.6-litre Austin A90 engine and running gear – which explains why Healey, Jensen and Frazer Nash all built A90-powered prototypes at this time.

Neither the Jensen nor the Frazer Nash were all that well thought out, but there's no doubt that the Healey 100 project was always promising. It is worthy of reflection that if the Healey 100 had not been such a promising way of using redundant A90 power, and if it had not been such a good-looking car, MG's EX175 might have got the nod instead. And if that had happened, the TF would never have been built.

In fact it's a well known story, told often and needing no embellishment, although perhaps a little explanation: the unpalatable truth was that BMC had not arisen from a merger, but from a takeover of Nuffield by Austin, and Nuffield companies would henceforth always be underdogs. At this time, therefore, BMC's forward planning was dominated by one man, Len Lord, whose obvious strategy was to make Austin even more pivotal than it already was. Looking back to the 1950s, it is clear that wherever a decision had to be taken between rival Austin and Nuffield projects, then the Austin ideas were invariably chosen.

It was for all these reasons, I suspect, that Len Lord chose to back the Austin-Healey 100 project in favour of MG's EX175, especially as the Austin-Healey was all set to use Austin engines, transmissions and front suspension components. Incidentally, although all of us enthusiasts, writers and historians have accepted the stories of Len Lord choosing the Austin-Healey project just a few days before EX175 was offered for inspection, as BMC's boss, he must already have known of the new MG's existence – it could not have been a surprise to him. And if it had been,

then Tatlow and John Thornley deserved to have been sacked, because to produce such an important new prototype without letting their bosses know would have been unacceptable. In fact Thornley always seems to have been on excellent terms with Lord – which was more than could be said of other Nuffield Organization managers. From Thornley's point of view:

> I was about the only senior executive who never had a blazing row with Len Lord, because I was always pleased to see him. He'd come in unannounced at Abingdon, and I'd say 'Hello, come on in!' – that sort of approach. No one else talked to him like that, so he developed quite a soft spot for Abingdon – and that made a big difference. I never got the rough edge of his tongue at all ... He administered largely by guesswork, but had the habit of being rather more right than he was wrong. Even if it was only 51 per cent to 49 per cent, if you pursue that line for long enough it begins to show.

Decisions which seemed to go against Abingdon's interests were naturally resented, but there was never anything discriminatory or spiteful about them. Most of them, when viewed with hindsight, can be seen to have been well justified.

However, Tatlow, Thornley and their managers were devastated by Len Lord's abrupt dismissal of EX175 in October 1952. Furthermore, not only had Lord rejected the new car, he had also told them, in his typically graceless way, that they should go back to Abingdon and find ways of selling even more MGs.

For a company which had just pushed up annual MG production from 11,065 to 13,669, and TD production from 7,451 to 10,838 (which was then an annual record for an MG model), this was not going to be easy. Worse, dealers in North America were starting to find difficulty in selling the square-rigged TD, which had already been on the market for three full years. Besides, by the end of 1952 there was an air of panic at Abingdon because at the recent London Motor Show two new sports cars had appeared which, frankly, terrified MG's bosses with their implications. Although both were prototypes – one-offs, in fact, at that time – both were definite rivals. They did what EX175 had been intended to achieve: look modern, and offer top speeds of around 100mph (160km/h). Nor were

they underfinanced cars from tiny companies – so once any development problems were sorted out they would certainly become serious competition.

These cars were the original Austin-Healey 100, and Triumph's first thoughts about a new TR2, and it didn't matter that they were prototypes, and had much larger engines than the TD: even though they could not possibly go into series production until the summer of 1953, they both looked threatening – and even at that stage, too, their proposed selling prices looked dangerously competitive.

RE-STYLING THE TD

MG, now led by John Thornley (who became general manager in November 1952) had no time to hang around. It was not enough to point to the TD's success, and to that indefinable selling point 'Safety Fast': the fact was that within a year the new cars from Austin-Healey and Triumph might make the existing TD look antideluvian. Not only that, but the TD would seem to be – and moreover would be – a much slower car.

With virtually no backing for a new

John Thornley

It was not without reason that John Thornley became known as 'Mr MG'. An accountancy student, he arrived at Abingdon in 1931 as a 22-year-old assistant in the service department: he already owned an M-Type Midget, and had run the fledgling MG Car Club. Thornley was the sort of enthusiast who kept companies like MG ticking over happily: he became service manager in 1934, wrote a seminal book on MG engine-tuning called *Maintaining the Breed,* and then moved up to become MG's sales manager in 1947. BMC made him MG's general manager in 1952, following the retirement of Jack Tatlow – just in time to develop the TF series.

After the T-Series had been discontinued, he moved up further, to become MG's managing director in 1957, holding that position until 1969 when he retired, glad to get away from the increasingly hostile and political atmosphere which followed the foundation of British Leyland. He died in 1994.

Another of the Palmer-Car styles would have had a modern nose and full width sides, while retaining a traditional MG grille. It is easy to scoff today, but BMC treated it seriously at the time.

This was the prototype TF, as mocked up in a matter of days at Abingdon in 1953. Compared with the TF which eventually went on sale, it had a different pattern of vents around the engine bay, including rows along the top of the bonnet which were not, in fact, required. [David Knowles]

model – especially from Cowley, where design work would have to be carried out – but with the urgent need to do something, the team set about facelifting the TD. While John Thornley knew exactly what was going on, he left Enever, Cecil Cousins and their tiny team to work a miracle. And although time was short, and capital for new tooling even shorter, he made clear that he wanted to see something new. So armed with a TD, their own ideas, some sheet metal, and the indispensable talents of Freddie Wake, Bert Wirdnam and a panel beater called Billy Wilkins, the team set out on a transformation. There was no question of making drawings – the changes were converted straight from 'good idea' to sheet metal.

Not without trauma and problems, the work was completed in just two weeks: finished in blue cellulose, the very first car was ready to show to the BMC board in January 1953. At first this prototype was no more than a rebodied TD, for changes which would be made to the running gear had yet to be agreed, and the interior finalized. Before the board meeting – and before John Thornley saw it – there was only time to take the prototype for a dash up and down MG's traditional test route, to and from Marcham on the west side of Abingdon itself.

While leaving the main passenger compartment/centre section unchanged, the facelift gave the car a reshaped radiator grille, new front and rear wings, modified bonnet panels, and detail changes around the tail; these included a repositioned fuel tank. Cecil Cousins was full of praise for Billy Wilkins's sheet-metal skills: 'He literally hand-made the first set of wings out of a sheet of metal, to our idea – virtually made it, there wasn't a drawing or anything.'

In fact development chief Alec Hounslow recalls that there was nothing unique in this process: 'We never needed drawings: half our cars were made without drawings lousing you up. We used to give it [the prototype] to the drawing office so they could draw around it with their pencils...'

Yet this was much more than simply luck allied to horny-handed toil: in the same way that previous MGs such as the K3 Magnette or the PA had been shaped, this was a neat, elegant, carefully formed two-seater without a single jarring line. Abingdon's long-serving enthusiasts thought they knew what a car should look like – and they were usually correct. The only external details of the very first prototype to be changed were the two lines of louvres in the bonnet top which were deleted: not only did this save money, but it looked better, and there was no loss of cooling performance under the bonnet. Everything else – everything – made it to the production lines.

Right from the start, it seems, MG knew that it would need to choose a new name, for 'TD Mark II' had already been used, and 'TD Mark III' didn't sound right. It still needed to be a T-Series car, so 'TE' was the next obvious choice – but that name was almost instantly discarded as being too close to 'Tee Hee', with its close links to children's humour. So it became the TF, also known as 'Abingdon's EX177'. Once the BMC had given their approval, this new project was officially 'adopted' by the body drawing office at Cowley where they called it D01047, and the sheet-metal changes were laboriously drawn up. In the meantime (and well ahead of the completion of these drawings) the Morris Bodies branch in Coventry started preparing the complete bodyshells.

This was the final flowering of the T-Series pedigree, a car where body and style changes took precedence over improvements to the running gear. At the front end, every change was affected by the use of a lower, and sloping-back radiator shell, the top of which was 3.5in (8.9cm) lower than that of the TD (and which used Riley RM-Series grille slats). This meant that new engine bay/bonnet panels would be needed, and of course it also encouraged the reshaping and lowering of the front wings; and for the very first time, too, this was an MG sports car with faired-in sealed-beam headlamps. This was the sheet metalwork of which Billy Wilkins could be most proud: it looked good then, and it still looks good today. In the same area, however, there was also a definite backward step, for this was the first MG in which the flat, louvred, engine-bay side panels were fixed in place; this meant that access to the engine itself (for service and repairs) would be restricted.

The body's TD-based centre section was not changed – importantly, this left the existing jigging, and the wooden skeleton, just as they were – this ensuring that Morris Bodies did not have to process a wholesale carve-up of its jigging arrangements, nor spend more money on new press tools for this part of the bodyshell.

Changes at the rear centred around the new and rather more sloping fuel tank – 12 galls/55 litres for the TF in place of 12½ galls/57 litres for the old TD, incidentally – which meant that the spare wheel sloped forward more than before; and to turn all this into an harmonious assembly, there were new rear-wing pressings with an emphasized flare at their tips. The number plate was also repositioned – it now lay above and along the bumper, rather than as a square plate alongside the fuel tank – as were the combined circular stop lamp/turn indicators, now on the rear wings themselves. All this was visually obvious, but most people didn't notice the

reshaping of the soft-top's frame, which was slightly lower than before, and the fact that the windscreen wiper motor had finally disappeared from view, under the scuttle; the wipers were now pivoted from the scuttle rather than from the top rail of the windscreen.

The overall effect of all these changes, and particularly that of the more rakish rear wing pressings, was a car slightly longer and wider than before, but with the same basic cockpit space.

Inside the car, too, there was an equally thorough facelift and package of improvements, which centred around a new facia panel. For the TF, the instrument dials were grouped into a centre facia panel with octagonal-styled instruments, flanked by open cubby boxes at either side. Although this was a neat arrangement, and one which did not have to be 'handed' for left- or right-hand-drive cars – and although it was another 'first' for Abingdon – it was also a step backwards. Most early Midgets, and every previous T-Series car, had had their rev counters placed ahead of the driver's eyes, while on the TD the rev-counter and the speedometer were in that location. But no matter which side the steering wheel was placed on the TF, the main instruments were always a long way out of the line of sight, except for the rev-counter which at least was placed as close as possible to the wheel, being 'handed' in the production process. Incidentally, even after all those years, there was still no fuel gauge...

Moving the windscreen wiper motor, though, was a definite advance, not only for function and visibility reasons, but with safety in mind. From the first TA of 1936 to the last TD of 1953, the wiper motor had always been placed on the inside of the top screen rail with the wipers themselves hanging down. The motor was of a type which allowed manual actuation in case of failure – and being a Joseph Lucas component, failures were not unknown ... This was also the very first T-Series Midget to be given individually adjustable seats; the telescopic steering column was retained; and there was a neat crash roll around the perimeter of the facia panel assembly.

Aerodynamically, of course, these changes made very little difference, for although the nose had been lowered a little and the headlamps faired-in, the windscreen still stood up as high and as proudly as before. Even though it was possible to fold the screen forward, just as it had been on other T-Series cars, the TF would still struggle against the wind.

RUNNING GEAR: TD UPDATES

Because there was very little money and no time to spare, the TF's chassis had to be based on that of the late-model TD. Except for the use of optional centre-lock wire wheels (at last!), a TD would find the TF altogether familiar, because modifications and improvements were confined to slight engine changes and a reversion to the 4.875:1 rear axle ratio last seen on TD Mk IIs and (in the late 1930s) on the TA.

The chassis frame, the general layout, the front and rear suspensions, steering and brakes were all as before, which meant that there was not likely to be any hiccup at Abingdon in changing over from one model (the TD) to the next (TF). As already discussed in Chapter 5, centre-lock wire wheels had never been available on the TD as a production line item – no one understood why, at that time, and it was never properly explained – so it was a relief to see that these would figure on the TF.

The TF's rolling chassis was obviously based on that of the late-model TD, but there was a new grille style, the first-ever on a sporting MG which sloped backwards.

Compared with the last of the TDs, the TF's 1,250cc engine produced 57bhp instead of 54bhp, with 65lb/ft of peak torque instead of 64lb/ft, much of this improvement being due to the adoption of the Mk II's 8.0:1 compression ratio and larger SU carburettors, and the use of a pair of pancake air cleaners; these were made necessary by the confines of the latest body and engine bay panelling, because it was impossible to squeeze the bulky 'pancake' cleaner from the TD into the space available.

By this time, please note, the XPAG engine was really living on borrowed time, as the MG YB saloon was about to be discontinued, and the only other car within BMC therefore still using a version of the unit was the single-carburettor Wolseley 4/44 – and BMC was already planning to update that car with a BMC B-Series engine.

Another novelty which MG never publicized, was that the TF was also to be the first T-Series sports car to use a 'dummy' water radiator filler cap. All previous T-Series cars had used a real radiator and a real filler, but the TF was given a separate radiator, concealed behind the leant-back brightwork grille.

THE TF INTO PRODUCTION

By modern standards, the pre-production work which went into proving the TF's

The only way to identify this TF chassis from that of a late-model TD is by the different carburettor layout, with sloping air-cleaners.

design was laughably small. The very first car, which carried the chassis no. TD3/26849 and was really no more than a rebodied TD, was cobbled up by January 1953. The only official TF pre-production car, which carried the once-traditional chassis number of TF 0251 (as well as TD2/29748), first ran in mid-August 1953, having been assembled among the last 200 TDs to be built.

After the very last TD was assembled on 17 August, there was a short delay for re-tooling, particularly at the Morris Bodies branch in Coventry, while arrangements were made to assemble the new-shape front and rear ends of the bodyshell. After two weeks, the first nine TFs started assembly at Abingdon (actually on 3 September 1953): in fact the first two cars were not finished until 17 September, with five more completed the day after – at which point the flood of new cars began.

BMC, incidentally, swept away one piece of tradition at this point, insisting that the TF production sequence begin at chassis No. 501, this being the original home-market spec example.

(This must have been a very thin time for Abingdon's workforce: even though it was summer-holiday time, this was the point when the last of the YB saloons was being built, and when the very last Riley RM-Series 2 $1/_2$-litre models moved down the lines. So for a time in August/ September 1953, the assemblies would have been virtually empty.)

Fate always conspired against the TF ever getting its fair share of publicity, because when the time came to launch the car, in mid-October 1953, the all-new Magnette ZA saloon received much more attention. Even so, *The Motor* welcomed the TF as being 'faster and better-looking', also stating that: '...the MG Midget open

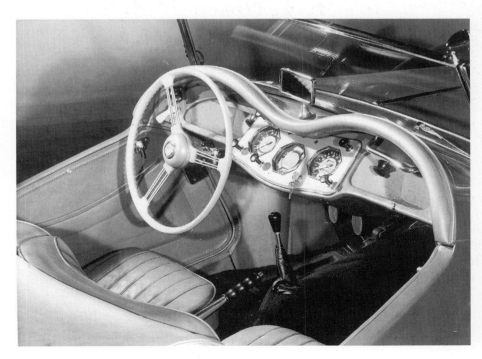

For the TF, Abingdon was allowed to develop a new style of facia, with octagonal-rimmed instruments mounted on a central panel. The vast majority of all TFs were built with left-hand drive, like this car, for export to North America.

147

For MG, the style of the TF was a big step forwards – though it was not as radical as they would have liked. This was the very first MG sports car to have sealed beam headlamps partly recessed into the front wings.

sports two-seater has been very much improved for 1954. It is not losing the classic lines which have endeared TC- and TD-series cars to so many Americans, yet it has been subtly modernized in appearance.' *The Autocar* was equally diplomatic, for it pointed out that:

The MG Midget is a car that, probably, has changed less in outward appearance than any other model over the same period of time ... By these remarks it is not meant to imply that design has remained static since the first MG Midget was produced very many years ago; nothing could be further from the truth ... even now the recently introduced TF model shows that the bodywork has been restyled to produce a much cleaner external appearance though retaining the MG Midget characteristics...

The TF and its Rivals in the UK, 1935 to 1955

Even before the TF was announced, MG must have known that it would face really tough competition because for the first time there were larger and faster cars selling at prices much closer to that of the TF. Here is how the obvious competition lined up at the end of 1953:

Jowett Jupiter (1,486cc)	£1,028.21
MG TF (1,250cc)	**£780.29**
Morgan Plus 4 (2,088cc) **	£801.54
Triumph TR2 (1,991cc)	£787.38

** The 90bhp/1,991cc/TR2-engined Plus 4 would appear within a year.

Although the ancient HRG and Singer Roadster models were still listed, they had become totally uncompetitive; but now the TF faced really serious competition from the new Triumph TR2. The latter might still have been somewhat rough-and-ready at the time, but it sold at nearly the same price as the TF, and was a 100mph (160km/h) machine.

In a later issue, the magazine commented that: 'From "sitting down" for many years, the Midget seems to have adopted a crouching position, with a subtle suggestion of extra liveliness.' Road tests did not follow these announcements, however, and they would have told BMC-watchers that the TF was, indeed, little faster than the TD. It was only in the USA where the vast majority of all Midgets were to be sold, that any authentic figures were ever taken.

Although the TF got off to an encouraging start – the thousandth car was completed on 7 December 1953 – in the UK there was no doubt that it was going to face a pricing problem in the market place. The last of the TDs had been priced at £752, the first of the TFs cost £780 – but the 105mph (169km/h)/2-litre Triumph TR2, which was just going into series production, was labelled at £787. Similar price comparisons applied in the USA, so would MG's traditional customers be tempted away to Triumph at such an attractive price, even though the Coventry-built machine still had no pedigree?

No one at Abingdon seems to have expected the TF to have a long life, as the original plan for the production cars only ordered up 7,000 parts; at the original rate this number of cars might have been completed well before the end of 1954. Because the newly announced MG Magnette and Riley Pathfinder saloons were late getting into production, Abingdon concentrated on the TF for a time, making at least 200 cars a week during the winter of 1953/1954. In those first few months, the vast majority of all TFs being built were left-hand-drive machines for the USA market, and well over half of them were fitted with wire wheels. By the end of the year, 1,114 TFs had already been exported, of which most were on their way to the USA, besides 327 to Europe, 20 to Australia and 12 to Canada.

At this time a handful of specially equipped cars were made, the production records sometimes quoting a higher (4.55:1) rear axle ratio and a 'special engine'. Both this axle and the TD-type 5.125:1 rear axle ratio were, in any case, quoted as options. Early in 1954, however, John Thornley and his colleagues had to accept a rather unpalatable truth: that the TF really wasn't selling as rapidly as had been hoped. Sales, particularly in the USA, were well down on those once achieved by the TD, and Stateside tests had been positively lukewarm. In its March 1954 issue, for instance, *Road & Track* headlined a test of the $2,260 as 'America's Best Sports Car Buy', and had this to say:

> Of all the cars which we have occasion to drive there is one above all others which, by its every characteristic, clearly defines the term 'sports car'. To drive an MG is sheer pleasure. This is no car for the average Joe looking for transportation. Only those who know and appreciate the fun of driving a car which responds to skilful handling will ever get to like an MG...the fact remains that the entire staff of *Road & Track* vied with each other to produce the best reason for using the MG.

That was the good news. The bad news was that: '...the new TF is an anomaly – a retrogression. The revised styling, though lower and more rakish, is still far from being modern, and the performance is well below the 1954 Detroit norm...' No one at MG could be blamed for either of these shortcomings; the car's general handling, response and overall character were fine, but the problems were interlinked, and had been imposed on the marque by BMC chairman Len Lord's attitude in 1952. It must have been galling to see, at exactly the time the TF started to suffer, that Lord became Sir Leonard. Someone, if not MG managers, was obviously grateful to him for something!

Although there was no panic, something had to be done, and quickly. Nothing at all could be changed to affect the style, nor the car's weight, so all efforts went into boosting its performance – and even then the

This side view of the TF summarizes the changes from the TD. Around an unchanged TD centre section, MG produced a sloping bonnet, new wings and a new sloping-back radiator grille, while the tail end was made rather more rakish, to suit. The TF was also given optional wire wheels, which the TD had always lacked.

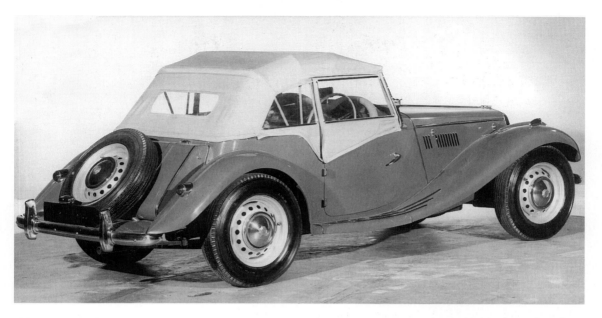

The TF from three-quarter rear, in basic steel-disc wheeled form, showing the more sloping fuel tank arrangement, and the re-detailed rear wings. The main section of the car, however, was that of the TD.

improvements would always be limited by the rather poor aerodynamics. Briefly – very briefly no doubt – thought was given to fitting a version of the new ZA Magnette's BMC B-Series engine and transmission, but as this assembly was heavier and bulkier it would almost certainly have involved making changes to the chassis, and it would probably have destroyed the TF's extremely good overall balance. No such car, as far as I know, was ever built, although a further development of that idea was responsible for the creation of the Naylor TF1700 of the 1980s.

Change could only come from the existing hardware. Fortunately for MG, an enlarged version of the 1,250cc XPAG engine – the 1,466cc XPEG derivative – had been in existence for some time at the Morris Engines plant at Courthouse Green. Internal politics – which might otherwise

be interpreted as 'jealousy from Longbridge' – had prevented the enlarged unit from being used in any previous Nuffield/BMC car – it would, for instance, have been ideal in the underpowered Wolseley 4/44 saloon – though it was already fully developed. MG engineers knew it by their own project code of EX176.

This enlargement was, in fact, a fairly major carve-up of the existing design. The original cylinder block casting did not have much spare 'meat' around the bores, and to increase that cylinder bore from 66.5mm (1,250cc engine) to 72mm (1,466c engine) – only 5.5mm/0.22in – meant that the block had to be recored. Because no changes were made to the engine's top end – specifically, none to the porting, nor to the camshaft timing – the improvements were rather muted: although the 17 per cent capacity increase resulted in a 17 per cent torque

151

Model	Peak Power	Peak Torque
1,250cc (XPAG)	57bhp @ 5,500rpm	65 lb/ft @ 3,000rpm
1,466cc (XPEG)	63bhp @ 5,000rpm	76 lb/ft @ 3,000rpm

improvement, top end power went up by only 10 per cent.

As recorded in the previous chapter, a super-tuned (84bhp) version of the 1,466cc engine was proved at Utah in August 1954, when the new MG EX179 record car reached 153.69mph (247.29km/h). Except to admit that this was a larger version of the existing engine, MG publicists made little of the 1,466cc engine, and certainly did not suggest that it was about to be fitted to the later-model TFs.

TF1500: UNSUNG HERO

The second-generation TF, which was actually badged 'TF1500' by small plaques on either side of bonnet, went into production in July 1954, but what followed was a mystery. Not only was there something of a production mix-up, with both types of car being built for the next two months, but as far as I can see, the existence of the TF1500 was never really publicized, not even in the USA, when a help to the car's image was needed so much.

To give you an idea of the way posterity was to be confused, the very first TF1500 carried chassis number 6501, whereas the very last TF1250 carried chassis number 6950, and at any time both types were hopelessly intermingled on the final assembly lines. This is how the rather muddled changeover took place:

Chassis nos	Engines fitted	Final assembly dates
501 to 6500	XPAG, 1,250cc	16 Sept 1953 to 14 July 1954
6501 to 6650	XPEG, 1,466cc	21 July 1954 to 26 August 1954
6651 to 6750	XPAG, 1,250cc	10 Aug 1954 to 26 August 1954
6751 to 6850	XPEG, 1,466cc	26 Aug 1954 to 10 Sept 1954
6851 to 6950	XPAG, 1,250cc	26 Aug 1954 to 22 Sept 1954
6951 onwards	XPEG, 1,466cc	From 10 Sep 1954

By the time an owner had specified the centre-lock wire wheels and the optional accessory luggage grid, the tail of the TF was beginning to look distinctly 'busy'.

Most of the new TF1500s were intended for sale in the USA, although the first cars did not reach that continent until September 1954, when they became rather 'hush-hush' 1955-model-year cars! The TF1500 was never officially announced in the UK, although some cars were sold here, and it was never exported to Australia or to Canada. Furthermore I have checked and rechecked in Britain's motoring magazines, and I suspect than no mention of an enlarged-engined TF was ever made. The mystery, however, deepens, because both the TFs produced for display at the London Motor Show of October 1954 – carrying chassis numbers 7252 and 7253 – had 1,466cc engines, yet neither seems to have had 'TF1500' badges at the time, and were certainly not identified as such!

Years later, in a letter to a later owner of one of the cars, the wholesale manager of University Motors wrote about the example carrying chassis number 7253, confirming its identity: 'The MG TF1500 you have was indeed an Earl's Court Show model which was purchased by us at the end of the show in October 1954 and used as a demonstrator car until June 1955...'

For the TF, MG redesigned the carburettor air-cleaner arrangement, so that these could still be accommodated inside the more sloping bonnet lines. The gear-lever extension was the same as had been used on the TD model.

LAST CALL FOR THE TF

By the mid-1950s, MG had been under the thumb of Nuffield, or later BMC, for far too long. Not since 1935 had MG been able to make its own strategic decisions, and worse, it had never been able to conceive its own new models: the birth of each and every one of the T-Series models had been influenced elsewhere. For a brief period in 1952 it looked as if EX175 – a Thornley/Enever concept at Abingdon – might eventually dislodge the T-Series by 1953, but BMC's Len Lord put paid to that idea. That style and design, however, were too good to be abandoned, and in mid-1954 it would finally be revived: with a new

BMC engine/transmission line-up, it would become the MGA, and it would take over from the last of the TFs as soon as development and tooling were complete.

This was the point at which MG metaphorically washed its corporate hands of the T-Series cars. Once design and development work began on the MGA, there was no more time for the TF, so once the TF1500 had been finalized, the T-Series story began to wind down – from that moment the T-Series effectively became a 'yesterday's car'. About 6,500 cars had already been built by the time this model passed its first anniversary, and nearly 8,200 cars were complete before the end of the calendar year.

By the end of 1954, MG's planners were already hoping to start building MGAs by April 1955 (with an immediate public launch), which explains why a team of MGAs was entered for the Le Mans Twenty-Four Hours' race in June. Originally these were to have raced as early production cars, which would have been excellent publicity for the marque; however, due to a variety of delays and changes in finalizing press tools, the production tooling was not complete, so they had to appear as EX182 'specials' instead. In June 1955 *The Autocar*, loyally discreet to the last, merely wrote that:

The [EX182] car has been built to provide

information for a production version. Thus the general design, materials, and method of construction could be reproduced in quantity and the resultant vehicle would sell at a reasonable price...

By the end of 1954, in any case, the T-Series had been condemned to an early death. A look at MG's EX-register shows that there had been no new activity on T-Series cars after EX177 (which gave credibility to the Cousins/Hounslow/Wake TF lash-up of early 1953), and we also know that from mid-1954, TF assembly at Abingdon had been calculated to run down in April 1955, just ahead of the first of the MGAs. In fact the British motor industry's

In 1977 Leyland Cars circulated this picture of its latest model MGB GT, along with a TF owned by the British Motor Industry Heritage Trust. In only twenty-five years, it seems, all family resemblance had been lost.

'sanction' system of ordering and production planning made sure of that: in 'industry-speak', a 'sanction' was the planning approval given for a particular number of cars, chassis or engines to be built, and after that it was extremely difficult (and usually immensely costly) for that number to be varied.

According to the records that remain, in 1953 the original TF chassis 'sanction' was for 7,000 cars; this was increased to 10,000 in February 1954, then reduced to 9,200 in October 1954, but almost immediately stretched to 9,600 in November 1954. After that, with MGA preparations coming on apace, there were no further adjustments. As far as the TF was concerned, it was really the 'sanction' of 3,400 1,466cc XPEG engines from Courthouse Green, Coventry, and of a total of 9,600 bodyshells from the Morris Bodies branch, also of Coventry, which sealed the old car's fate: when the last body and the last engine were fitted together at Abingdon, that would also spell

This aerial view shows MG's Abingdon factory in its 1950s/1960s state, still recognizably developed from the Pavlova works, but with a line of extra bays added during and after the war. T-Series assembly was always concentrated in the factory blocks close to the main road in the foreground of this picture. Although some evidence of it remains today, much of the complex was bulldozed in the 1980s, and has been submerged under a trading estate.

the end for the TF. In fact by the end of 1954 the last of the TF1250s was long gone, and a total of just 1,951 TF1500s had been built, almost all of them destined for sale in North America. Only 1,449 true 'calendar year 1955' TFs remained to be built.

In 1955 only two oddities seem to have been produced, both of them in February 1955: one, chassis no. 9206, was noted as a 'competition car' (it was in fact the 'works' TF used by Pat Moss in the RAC International rally); and the other (chassis no. 9417) was recorded as having a 4.55:1 axle ratio (which was higher gearing than normal) and a tuned engine. These were delivered to the newly formed competitions department for use in rallies during the year. A total of eighteen TFs were produced on 3 January 1955, and assembly of the last thousand began on 27 January; and the last of all was completed on 12 April 1955, leaving for its customer a day later. Without ceremony – and certainly without any public announcement from the BMC press office – the TF's production career came to end. Because it was not yet ready to launch the TF's replacement, the MGA, BMC kept up the pretence that the TF was still in production for five more months, keeping the car in the price lists and saying nothing definite about its successor. Behind the scenes, however, all traces of T-Series production rapidly disappeared.

For several months, in fact, there was no evidence of sports cars at Abingdon, where the workforce had to fill in by building more of the other models which were already in residence – namely the last few of the 1½-litre engined Riley RM saloons, the Riley Pathfinder, and a growing number of MG ZA Magnettes. The fact that 230 per cent more Magnettes – 8,927 of them – were produced in 1955 than in 1954 proves its own point. Fortunately the simple assembly 'runways' at Abingdon could cope with any number of different models, whereas the T-Series facilities at the Morris Bodies branch in Coventry, such as they were, were cleared out to make way for the more lavish jigging and framing fixtures needed to built MGA shells.

It was unfortunate that because of the delay in announcing the MGA, the demise of the TF could not be publically noted. Its going also marked the end of an entire era at Abingdon: from 1929, when the first M-Type Midgets and 18/80s were being built in the converted leather-goods factory, to 1955 and the last of the TFs, every octagon-badged MG sports car had been of the same basic type – separate chassis, wooden-framed bodyshell, proud radiator style. We would never see that type of sports car again, because the MGA which took over in September was an entirely different machine.

TF (1953 – 1955)

Numbers built
9,600
Production period: TF1250: September 1953 to September 1954
                      TF1500: July 1954 – April 1955

Layout
Ladder-type separate steel chassis frame, with steel panelled body panels on a wooden bodyshell skeleton. Two-door, front engine/rear drive, sold as a two-seater open sports car.
Note: Where they differ, figures for the TF1500 are shown below in square brackets.

Engine
Type	Nuffield, Type XPAG [XPEG]
Block material	Cast iron
Head material	Cast iron
Cylinders	4 in-line
Cooling	Water
Bore and stroke	66.5 x 90mm [72 x 90mm]
Capacity	1,250cc [1,466cc]
Main bearings	3
Valves	2 per cylinder, operated by in-line overhead valves, pushrods and rockers, with camshaft mounted in block, driven by chain from crankshaft
Compression ratio	8.0:1 [8.3:1]
Carburettors	2 SU
Max. power	57bhp @ 5,500rpm [63bhp @ 5,000rpm]
Max. torque	65lb ft @ 3,000rpm [76lb ft @ 3,000rpm]

Transmission
Four-speed manual gearbox, with synchromesh on top, third and second gears
Clutch   Single dry plate

Overall gearbox ratios
Top	4.875
3rd	6.752
2nd	10.09
1st	17.06
Reverse	17.06
Final drive	4.875:1 (hypoid bevel)

15.25mph (24.54km/h)/1,000rpm in top gear

Suspension and steering
Front	Independent, by coil springs, wishbones, and hydraulic lever-arm dampers
Rear	Live (beam) axle, with half-elliptic leaf springs and Luvax hydraulic lever-arm dampers
Steering	Rack-and-pinion

Tyres	5.50-15in cross-ply
Wheels	Steel disc, bolt-on fixing, or optional centre-lock wire spoke
Rim width	4.0in

Brakes

| Type | Drum brakes at front, drums at rear, hydraulically operated |
| Size | 9 x 1.5in front and rear drums |

Dimensions (in/mm)

Track	
Front	47.4/1,204mm
Rear	50/1,270mm
Wheelbase	94/2,388mm
Overall length	147/3,734mm
Overall width	59.7/1,516mm
Overall height	
(hood erect)	52.5/1,334mm
Unladen weight	1,930lb/875kg

UK retail price

| At launch in 1953: | £780.29 (basic price £550) |

USA retail price

| In 1954 (and 1955): | $2,250   [$1,995] |

8   Today's T-Series

Until the 1960s, T-Series cars were to be seen in regular use on the roads, and one certainly expected to see a number of them in the car parks of major sporting events; however, those days are long gone, and only a confirmed traditionalist would use a T-Series MG for his daily transport these days. So it might be assumed that the world's stock are all kept as hobby-cars, for occasional use. By any standards, therefore, as the millenium approaches a T-Series is truly a classic car: to be used at leisure, for enjoyment, often kept in the best possible condition, and rarely maltreated or neglected. Are these truisms? I don't think so – and for enthusiasts wanting to join the ranks of T-series owners, that has to be good news.

Twenty years ago perhaps, and thirty years ago for sure, it was normal to see scruffy, down-at-heel T-Series cars being bought and sold for trivial money – but not any more. My own experience bears this out. The first car I ever bought, in 1960, was a TA which cost me £225; it blew its big end bearings within a month, and realized only £175 when I eventually traded it in against a modern saloon car. No, you couldn't do that any more. In fact today, the stock of good condition (or in 'antiques' terms, fine condition) T-Series cars is higher than ever, and except for the TBs and the Tickford-bodied cars of the late 1930s, there should always be a good choice on the market, more than for a long time.

Moreover when you have read the rest of this book, I hope you will have found out which model suits you, and what character appeals most – after which you will go out and buy one, and enjoy it!

Although it is easier to rebuild and maintain a T-Series MG than it was thirty years ago, no owner – and certainly no prospective new owner – should ever let themselves become complacent. Parts, expertise and records may be more freely available than at any time since the cars were superseded by MGAs and MGBs, but this does not mean that keeping a T-Series is cheap and cheerful. The secret is in the numbers, which speak for themselves: although more than 500,000 MGBs were built between 1962 and 1980, a mere 52,646 T-types were built in a couple of decades from 1936 to 1955. For that reason it simply hasn't made sense for specialist suppliers to invest as heavily in remanufacture and rebuilding of parts.

It can be done, however, as it is in the USA, in particular, where many of the new cars were sold, and where many now remain. Although new castings for items such as cylinder blocks, cylinder heads and gearbox casings are no longer available, it is usually possible to rebuild the running gear of the cars. Chassis frames can be reconstructed, and complete new bodyshells – or sections of shells – are all available.

This doesn't mean that you can rush into

This display of parts shows that all manner of replacements are available for the T-Series cars, including floorboards and seating. [Magna Press]

buying a car, or that you should pay good money for the very first glossy-looking T-Series car you are offered. Some years ago I actually explained why, and I think it still applies:

> It goes without saying, I hope, that there is no foolproof way to search for and find the T-Series car of your choice, either for enjoyment or for general use. I have seen far too many enormously expensive T-

Series cars which have included botched repair and restoration under a glossy skin – and I have also seen early T-Series cars sold, unrestored, at remarkably reasonable prices.

SURVIVORS

I don't have a world-wide register, so I can't tell you how many T-Series cars survive, or where they all are. And even if you did have such a record, wherever you live, and however you count them, you'd only find a tiny percentage of the cars built or exported. Statistically, British readers and those living in Commonwealth countries such as Australia, New Zealand and South Africa face real shortages. Figures tabulated on other pages show that nearly 90 per cent of Abingdon's T-series output went overseas, and that more than half the cars went to the USA, as did no less than 76 per cent of the later TD/TF types.

Although there has been some cross-border (and trans-ocean) trading since then (quite a number have been re-imported from the USA, especially if those cars have spent their lives in the southern 'dry' states of the Union), I think we can assume that a majority of the survivors are still in the USA, where all the TD/TF types will have left-hand drive. Interest in the cars is strong in the aforementioned countries, but very few (relatively speaking) now remain in Europe, and in other world territories where MG's presence was always limited.

Although I have not personally seen either of the TA Airlines (I believe both have been scrapped), examples of every other type survive, sometimes in surprising quantities (far more TA/TB Tickfords, for instance, are still in use today than you could ever have expected). What you choose, therefore, and why you choose one, becomes a matter of personal preference rather than of availability.

I am often asked for my own preferences, and I don't like to answer because if I tell the truth – and I will – it is bound to alienate other people. Nonetheless, I have committed myself as follows:

The TA

Although the TA was 'the original', I did not admire its specification as much as that of later types, mainly because of the rock-hard ride, and because of the ageing pedigree of the engine itself. The 1,292cc unit, with its long stroke and its crankshaft lacking counter-balance weights, never felt as smooth to me, and history shows us that it was not ultimately as tuneable as the later XPAG types. Even so, this was the first T-Series I bought. I liked the style, and I liked the traditional character – but in spite of this I was more impressed by the TB.

The TB

I don't have much experience of TBs (there were, after all, only 379 of them), but I would expect one to feel just like a post-war TC. Without trying one, don't dismiss the cockpit as being too narrow. As you will see from my comments in Chapter 4, I am not convinced that there is much difference between TB and TC cockpit space anyway, not if you believe a tape measure instead of paper claims. The big advance of the TB over the TA was, of course, the engine, and I'm sure I don't have to convince any T-Series lover about that.

In both cases, by the way, I love the Tickford derivative – to me, a TB Tickford is probably the most desirable of the pre-war T-Series cars, because it combines sporting character with real up-market comfort, though it is a little snug for some tastes. Maybe my preference for wind-up windows and a bit of wood decoration around the cabin tells you about me, if not about the cars...

The TC

Everything I have said about the TB applies to the TC. I can see why it sold so well, and why it has so many followers today – but I can also see why MG was so ready to replace it by the TD in 1950. When I was very young I was more attracted by TR2s and 100/4s, but that was because I was dazzled by a modern style. Looking back, I can now see that the TC was the best of the truly traditional MGs, a bit more roomy than the others, a bit more softly sprung (but only just !) – and a bit more easily available.

By this time, though, I'd got tired of the way the tall thin wheels reacted to bumpy roads, and to the vagaries of the steering, particularly as it wore when getting old. Certainly as a piece of engineering, the TC was vastly inferior to the TD.

The TD

Abingdon did a good job here, in re-inventing a great pedigree without losing control.

Maybe the TD wasn't any faster than the TC, but it was very much more comfortable, it handled better, steered better, and it seemed to be a lot more spacious. All in all, the TD was very cleverly done: if you were a traditionalist you never complained about the style. If you liked modern engineering, you loved the Issigonis-inspired independent front end and the rack-and-pinion steering. But if you whinged that the TD had 'gone soft', then I think you needed to move up a decade or so – and if you didn't like the looks, you were obviously no longer a supporter of Abingdon's style anyway.

I agree with you about the wheels, though. Nuffield, later BMC, never gave us a convincing excuse for dropping the wire-wheel option – and anything they had claimed before 1953 was swept away when the option came back for the TF! On the

This shows the way in which all T-Series bodies (this is a TD) were built up on a wooden skeleton. After a great deal of abuse, neglect and assault from water and other filth, these components can rot badly, but replacements are all available. [Magna Press]

Although new castings are not available, almost everything needed to refurbish, rebuild and otherwise recreate a T-Series MG engine is available, as superlative concours cars continue to prove. Where originality is concerned, owners should always study contemporary photographs like this.

other hand, have you ever seen a TD retrofitted with TF wheels ? It looks slightly odd, somehow.

However, even though the TD was a lot better, overall, than the TC, it isn't my favourite T-Series.

The TF

I may surprise many people by choosing the TF as my favourite. As far as the chassis is concerned, there is nothing to choose between a TF and a TD (the wire wheels don't make any difference) – I just happen to prefer the style. The high speed experi-

mentation which resulted in the birth of the TF was nothing short of inspired, because to my mind it converted a rather severe, square-rig shape into something far more appealing. Away with those clichéd remarks about it being a 'TD that's been kicked in the face' or 'too little, too late': I think it is an elegant little car. The interior, in any case, is much the best of any T-Series (separate seats, at last!), and I still admire the complex curves surrounding the front wings, headlamps, and that sloping radiator grille.

When Alistair Naylor decided to build a 1980s 'replicar' as a clone of the T-Series, he chose the TF rather than the TD, and I could always see why. Did you ever think the proposed 'Palmer car' (see Chapter 7) was as pretty as a TF? Of course not...

PERFORMANCE

I hope you don't intend buying a T-Series as a high-performance sports car for the new millennium, because it certainly isn't that. A chassis which was competitive in the 1930s had begun to lag in the 1940s, and was, frankly, struggling to stay on terms in the 1950s. As long as you buy one for its character, its looks, and its out-and-out British-bulldog aura, you will not be disappointed. And you'll soon get used to being left standing at the traffic lights. It is hard to admit, but I've just looked up the published performance figures of current (1998) models, and found that the TF1250's 0–60mph (0–97km/h) time (about 19 seconds, two up, for a standard-engine type) is beaten by just about every 1998 model in the lists.

My reaction on the one hand is that you should certainly not be ashamed of this

Many of the trim, electrical and instrument details shown in this study of a TF can now be found from MG rebuilders. In any case, instruments can always be reconstructed (at a price). My advice is not to be tempted to build yourself a 'modified' version of Abingdon's best, as this policy actually detracts from its resale value.

fact, if only because car performance has improved dramatically in the last generation. On the other it is to remind you all that T-series performance is only a part of the charm of these cars. Maybe a TA/TB/TC is likely to be outpaced as regards handling, too – but with appropriate tyres fitted, any one of the TD/TF generation can handle as well as the best moderns.

There is one more 'plus'. How many modern cars – even modern sports cars – have the sheer charisma, the looks, and the feel of a well preserved T-Series?

PROBLEMS, PROBLEMS...

Nothing I could write here would increase the accepted knowledge of T-Series

problems and how to solve them, but I think it is worth summarizing the 'what to look for' advice.

If you are lucky enough to be able to afford a properly restored – or should I say, in some cases, recreated? – T-Series model, you may not have to worry about deterioration for many years to come because modern protective treatment, particularly of steel body panels and the wood framing to which they were attached, has improved enormously. Generally speaking, the running gear was always robust and reliable; however, new castings and forgings are no longer available for items such as cylinder blocks. To restore a car, therefore, repairs will have to take over from replacement in some areas – though it is much easier to find replacement items as various as

Rear axle detail of a TA – not to make any particular points about that car, but to prove the simplicity of the chassis engineering of all T-Series cars. Given time (and money!) it is always possible to recreate an early T-Series chassis.

engine valve gear, carburettors, gear wheels, brakes, dampers and road springs.

If you strip out a T-Series car for restoration by taking off the bodyshell, you will probably be encouraged by the simplicity of the rolling chassis you expose, how easy it seems to be to get at everything, and how straightforward a complete strip-down actually is. This, of course, is a tribute to Abingdon's design process – and it is also a reflection on the way the chassis were built up in the first place, with the very minimum of complex jigging and fixtures.

As far as the TA/TB/TC chassis is concerned, you will probably also be shocked by its obvious lack of rigidity and cross-bracing. This is because in the 1930s there was a widely held belief that springing should be hard, and that chassis frames should be slightly flexible; this didn't do much for the longevity of bolt-on bodyshells (which also had to flex, to suit), but it did make it cheap, quick and easy to tool up for a new model. This also explains why the only pressed sections of a TA/TB/TC frame were the longitudinal side members. At restoration time you may be glad of that, because it means that most of the rest of the frame – the bits that eventually rust away, or might have been destroyed in accident damage – are easy enough to fabricate and re-create.

TD/TF frames, on the other hand, are at once more robust and more difficult to restore. The good news is that because they are solid, they tend to last for many years, but the bad news is that restoration can be expensive.

Because the original bodyshells were built down to a price, and built very quickly (all except the Tickford and Airline types coming from the Morris Bodies branch in Coventry), they tended to deteriorate badly in all but very dry climates. Twenty years ago most of the world's stock of T-Series cars had very scruffy bodies, with rusty panelling and badly rotted wooden frames. However, in many cases these days, all that has changed. Replacement panels, wooden sections or complete bodyshells are now widely available (the one-make clubs – see below – will advise where to find them), and preservation techniques have improved dramatically, the result being that a well restored T-series body looks set to last for many years to come.

The problem with the wood skeleton around which the bodyshell was erected was that it was prone to attack from water, salt, stress and strain, and even (in some countries) infestation from destructive insects. Crumbling sections, sagging doors which no longer fitted their apertures, and bonnets almost impossible to align against bulkheads were all symptoms of worn-down bodies.

Today, of course, it is still possible to buy abandoned T-Series cars which demonstrate every possible body problem, but if the price is right, and the funds are available, it is always possible to 'make good', or even to fit completely new sections or shells. If, incidentally, some 'fitting', fettling or general adjustment is needed to make the new bits fit the original parts, don't despair: it was just the same when Abingdon was building hundreds of new cars every week!

Trim, carpets, seating, soft-tops, side curtains, wooden floor sections and every related body equipment item have also been remanufactured in recent years, these items often being built to higher standards than when the cars were new. It is quite acceptable, for instance, to specify soft-tops with a different material, which not only look good, but which will last longer. Originality ? Well, of course, that's up to you...

CLUBS

No matter in what country he lives, a T-Series owner will always be able to find a one-make club which caters for his needs. Because books stay in print for some time, yet club secretaries and their addresses seem to change frequently, I am often reluctant to publish contacts; however, in the case of the three British MG clubs I have no reservations.

MG Car Club Ltd
Kimber House,
P.O. Box 251,
Abingdon,
Oxon OX14 1FF
Tel : 01235-555552

This is the descendant of the original club, set up in 1930 with John Thornley as its organizing secretary. For many years it was both factory-backed and factory-located, but from 1969 it became totally independent. In many ways this is the most 'sporting-minded' of the British MG clubs, there being a thriving T-Series Register which not only looks after parts and rebuilding, but also motorsport of several types. In recent years strong links with the Rover Group have been maintained (now that the MGF is on the market, factory and club have a strong mutual interest). The club owns its own HQ, situated just yards from the historic old MG factory administration block; this is permanently staffed during office hours. The MG CC has branches all over the world, but I recommend that you contact HQ to obtain the latest details. Its regular magazine is called *Safety Fast.*

MG Owners' Club
Octagon House,
Station Road,
Swavesey,
Cambs CB4 5QZ
Tel: 01954-231125

Founded in 1973, the Owners' Club claims to be the largest one-make motor club in the UK, and caters for every type of MG ever built. Commercially very aggressive – it markets many of its own spare parts and accessories, and also has a thriving insurance scheme – it is much more involved in the restoration and maintenance of MGs, plus the social side, than in motorsport. Its membership is largely UK-based, and its large, glossy, monthly magazine is called *Enjoying MG.*

MG Octagon Car Club
Unit 1 and 2,
Parchfields Enterprise Park,
Colton Road,
Trent Valley,
Rugeley
Staffordshire WS15 3HB
Tel: 01889 574666

The third of the British MG clubs was set up in 1969, and has always specialized in the coverage of older MGs; it is not involved in MGAs, MGBs, Midgets and the like. For that reason it is the single most useful specialized club for owners of T-series cars. Known for its enthusiasm, and for its special interest in older-type MGs, the Octagon Club co-exists happily with its bigger rivals, who see it providing a different service from any that they can offer. Like the other clubs, there is a special interest in restoration and maintenance.

Appendix 1
Common Hardware

Without the resources of the Nuffield Organization, MG could never have built any of its T-Series models. Putting it bluntly, the MG business was always far too small for it to finance the development of its own engines and transmissions, and always had to rely on modifying those designed for more mundane mass-produced Morris or Wolseley family cars. Following is a record of where the basic hardware for the different types originated.

TYPE MPJG ENGINE: 1,292CC (USED IN THE TA)

The origins of this engine stretch back to 1919 (see panel on page 32) when Hotchkiss of Coventry began building side-valve engines with a 102mm stroke for the 'bullnose' Morris. The first overhead valve engine (which was also their final evolution) finally came along in 1936, when a 1,292cc version with a 63.5mm cylinder

Len Lord (left) was the architect of Nuffield's rationalization in the 1930s, and BMC's similar streamlining in the 1950s. Blame him if you wish, but I do believe that at the time it made a great deal of economic, if not emotional, sense.

bore, rated at 41bhp and known as an MPJW type, was fitted to the new Wolseley 10/40. The Morris Ten Series III (closely related to the Wolseley 10/4) came along in the autumn of 1937, this being the MPJM, with 37bhp. For the MG TA there was a tuned-up version of the engine known as the MPJG; complete with twin SU carburettors, this was rated at 51bhp.

As far as MG models were concerned, this 1,292cc engine went out of use during 1939; the other cars which used the same family – the Morris Ten SIII and the Wolseley 10/40 – had been dropped earlier, in 1938.

Note that there was also a larger version of this overhead-valve four-cylinder engine. A 1,548cc engine with a 69.5mm bore was not only fitted to the Morris Twelve SIII of 1937–39 and the Wolseley 12/48 SII and SIII of 1936–48, but was also used in the MG VA model of 1937–39, where it was rated at 54bhp.

To give you an idea of the extent to which product planning was alive and well in the Nuffield Organization at the time, six-cylinder engines of 1,818cc, 2,062cc, 2,288cc, 2,322cc and 2,561cc, all with the trademark 102mm stroke, were also made in the 1930s and 1940s, sharing many of the same components as the 'fours' – valve gear, connecting rods and lubrication details, for example. In addition to being used in several of the larger Morris and Wolseley types, such engines also found a home in the late-1930s MG SA and WA types.

TYPE XPAG AND XPEG: 1,250 AND 1,466CC (USED IN TB, TC, TD AND TF TYPES)

This was an all-new overhead valve engine, started in 1936, which was first introduced in 1938, originally in single-carburettor guise as the 37bhp XPJM of 1,140cc (63.5 x 90mm), to power the Morris Ten Series M. It was totally different from the old-fashioned MPJM which it effectively replaced: smaller, more than 60lb/27kg lighter, better-breathing and more fuel-efficient than before. The Wolseley Ten of 1939 was essentially the same car (but with a separate chassis instead of unit construction), and used the same 1,140cc engine.

In Morris and Wolseley form, this engine was used in the UK until the summer of 1948. It also featured in the Hindustan marque, which was an Indian version of the Morris Ten Series M.

The original MG version of this engine, coded XPAG, was an enlarged version with a wider cylinder bore (66.5 x 90mm, 1,250cc). Fitted to the TB, TC, TD and early TF sports cars, it was originally rated at 54bhp, but produced 57bhp in the TF1250. The same basic 1,250cc engine was also used in three post-war MG models and one Wolseley (known in this model as the XPAW). All but one of them used a redeveloped, 46bhp, single-carburettor version of the unit:

MG YA saloon	1,250cc	Single SU carb	46bhp
MG YT Tourer	1,250cc	Twin SU carbs (TC tune)	54bhp
MG YB saloon	1,250cc	Single SU carb	46bhp
- and -			
Wolseley 4/44	1,250cc	Single SU carb	46bhp

There was another MG connection with the Wolseley 4/44, whose basic monocoque, design, and style was also used in the MG Magnette ZA saloon, though that model used an entirely different type of BMC B-Series engine. By the mid-1950s, however, BMC policy on engine rationalization was well advanced, and for MG the last of these engines – the 1,466cc XPEG type – was built early in 1955, while the last 'XP' type of all – for the last of the Wolseley 4/44 saloons – was built in 1956.

FOUR-SPEED GEARBOX

The same basic four-speed gearbox was used in a whole variety of Morris, Wolseley and MG models from the 1930s to the 1950s, though there were any number of permutations – different sets of internal ratios, synchromesh and gearchange controls. Nowadays, no doubt, some fast-talking press-man would describe this as a 'medium-duty' transmission; Nuffield never bothered to describe it at all!

As with the various engines, this gearbox was originally developed for mass-production in Morris and Wolseley cars, usually to back the MPJM/MPJW or (later) the more modern XPJM/XPJW types; however, over the years it was developed so far, and in so many ways, that the gearbox used in the TF1500 was scarcely recognizable as a descendant of the original.

The very first such four-speed gearbox, with constant mesh (but not yet synchromesh) on top and third gears, appeared in the new-generation Morris Tens and the latest 1.55-litre Cowleys of September

Doesn't look promising, does it ? Under the skin of the 1939-model Morris Ten Series M, though, was the same basic engine and gearbox as would be used in the MG TB, TC, TD and TF series.

1932, having a cast-iron casing which was clearly related to that of all the T-Series sports cars which followed. In this guise it had a long, sturdy and direct-acting central gear-change lever, and there was a cork-faced clutch running in oil.

Synchromesh was added to top and third gears a year later, a dry-plate clutch was adopted for the TB and later types, and the same basic transmission was then fitted to various Tens, Twelves and Fourteens, together with their closely related Wolseleys and MGs, during the 1930s, and kept until they were discontinued in 1948.

Along the way, however, there were changes to the synchromesh arrangements and to the internal ratios themselves. The best way to sort these out is through the following table concerning MG models:

Model	Internal Gearbox Ratios	Comments
TA	1.00, 1.42, 2.20,3.715, reverse 4.78:1	No synchromesh. Only used on TAs up to engine number MPJG 683.
TA	1.00, 1.32, 2.04, 3.454, reverse 4.44:1	Synchromesh on top and third gears, used from engine number MPJG 684.
TB and TC	1.00, 1.35, 1.95, 3.38, reverse 3.38:1	Synchromesh on top, third and second gears.
TD and TF	1.00, 1.385, 2.07, 3.50, reverse 3.50:1	Synchromesh on top, third and second gears. Similar to TC/TD gearbox, but with new low-level remote control extension.
Related MG models		
SA	1.00, 1.38, 2.13, 3.76, reverse 4.76:1	No synchromesh for first few cars, but from mid-1936 all other cars with synchromesh on top and third gears. Same basic gearbox as TA model.
VA	1.00, 1.35, 1.95, 3.38, reverse 3.38:1	Synchromesh on top, third and second gears. Same basic gearbox as TB and TC models.

WA	1.00, 1.418, 2.155, 3.646, reverse 3.646	Synchromesh on top, third and second gears. Same basic gearbox as VA, and TB/TC models, but with different internal ratios.
YA, YB and YT	1.00, 1.385, 2.07, 3.50, reverse 3.50:1	Basic gearbox as TD/TF type, but with different gear selection arrangements.

Most of the Wolseley 4/44s, which were announced in 1952, may have rusted away, but their engines – single carburettor versions of the 1,250cc TD unit – may be worth rescuing.

Note: Although gearboxes fitted to the post-war Morris Oxford and Wolseley 4/50 ranges had the same internal ratios as the TD/TF types, these used different cast-iron casings, along with a steering-column gearchange. Although it used the same engine as the MG YA/YB model, the Wolseley 4/44 used even wider internal ratios, along with a Morris Oxford-based steering column gearchange.

Successors to the T-Series and YB models – the MGA and ZA Magnette respectively – used a new-generation BMC B-Series gearbox.

REAR AXLES/DIFFERENTIALS

The TA, TB and TC models all used the same basic design of Nuffield spiral bevel final drive – which is to say that the pinion gear was at the same level as the drive-shafts.

Because different Nuffield models used different rear track dimensions, only the differentials themselves were commonized, and even then it was only the smaller components – bearings, star wheels, bushes and related items – which were interchangeable. These were the ratios used, the difference being accomodated by different combinations of crown wheel, and pinion, teeth:

TA	4.875:1
TB and TC	5.125:1

Other Nuffield cars used:

4.75:1
4.778:1
5.143:1
5.22:1
5.286:1
5.333:1

The TD and TF models used a more modern type of Nuffield hypoid bevel final drive (introduced for the 1950s) – which is to say that the pinion gear was placed below the level of the drive shafts. These were the ratios used:

TF	4.875:1
TD	5.125:1

Other Nuffield cars used:

4.55:1

The successors to the T-Series and YB models – the MGA and the ZA Magnette respectively – used a new-generation B-Series axle.

Appendix 2
Naylor and Hutson: T-Series for the 1990s

One of the most intriguing cars to appear at the height of Britain's 'classic car boom' was Alistair Naylor's Naylor TF1700; this was a car that looked very similar to the MG TF, but which had many more modern features included in the body, and entirely different running gear. Although it was much faster than any TF, yet built equally as well, somehow it wasn't an MG – which was always the problem. At the time, it's

fair to say, the MG fraternity really didn't know what to think about this car. A good deal of controversy had already arisen over the building of classic 'replicas' – not least those of AC Cobras and Jaguar D-Types – so although Naylor was already a respected specialist, dealing with the remanufacture of parts for T-Series cars, many MG enthusiasts were ready to hate him for what he had done.

The Naylor TF1700 of the mid-1980s was visually almost identical with the real TF models, but underneath all was new.

When the TF1700 was previewed in 1984, Naylor Bros were wholly honest about it: although the body style looked like that of the 1955-type MG TF, it hid totally up-to-date running gear. Externally, the only quick way to 'pick' a Naylor TF1700 was by its different seats and facia style, the doors hinged at the front instead of the rear, and the different type of wire-spoke wheels, along with details such as indicators built into the bumpers, and different badging.

The interior and equipment was much more luxurious – and much more '1980s' – than any real TF had ever been, because the seats were real leather (by Callow &

Maddox), there was a wood-veneer dashboard, and a modern heating/vantilation system. On the other hand, there was no sign of any octagon-styled instruments, and that heating system had to live where the old-style toolbox had once been, which meant that the toolbox had been abandoned!

A new design of chassis frame followed the general lines of the original TF, but although the wheelbase and rear tracks were virtually the same as before, the front track was significantly wider: 52.2in (1,326mm) instead of 47.4in (1,204mm). One reason for that was because an MGB steering rack (rather

The new Naylor TF1700 factory in Bradford, being inaugurated by Jean Cook, daughter of MG founder Cecil Kimber.

longer than a TF rack) was used.

The Naylor TF1700 was only available in right-hand drive at first, and although Alistair Naylor talked of developing left-hand drive, particularly for cars sold in North America, he also admitted that it would be expensive to achieve – and it was not done.

Front suspension was by coil springs, double wishbones and an anti-roll bar, using some Morris Ital parts, and using telescopic dampers, while an Ital rear axle was sprung on coil springs, with radius arms, a Panhard rod and telescopic dampers looking after location.

The ride on early cars was extremely harsh, and there was tail-out oversteer when the car was driven hard; but work both by Lotus and by Armstrong Patents (damper specialists) improved this as production progressed. Ital-style brakes were also used: 9.9in front discs and 8.0in rear drums, with vacuum servo assistance.

Power was by a 1.7-litre British Leyland/Rover 0-Series engine, a 77bhp overhead-cam four-cylinder unit as used in contemporary cars like the Morris Ital and the Austin Ambassador, and it was backed by an all-synchromesh four-cylinder gearbox, also as used in the Ital.

Naylor announced that production had begun in January 1985, at a price set at £12,950, and the first deliveries were made in April. Chrome wire wheels cost £404.89, metallic paintwork £134.55, and a chrome luggage grid £57.50. At the time, it was said, the Bradford factory could produce up to 200 cars a year, though this rate was never even approached. PR and publicity statements, it has to be said, always raced well ahead of reality – but how often have we heard that before...?

Autocar magazine tested a production car in August 1985, discovering that although the TF1700 was considerably faster than the TF1250 (or even the TF1500) had ever been, there was the inescapable 'brick wall' effect of those awful aerodynamics. Here, for interest, is a brief performance comparison between the 1985 Naylor TF1700, and the authentic MG TF:

	Naylor TF1700	*TF1250*	*TF1500*
Top speed (mph)	89	80	85
0–60mph/97km/h (sec)	12.5	18.9	16.3
Standing 1/4-mile (sec)	19.5	21.6	20.7
Typical mpg	23–28	app. 26	N/A
Weight (lb/kg)	1,932/876	1,930/875	1,930/875
UK Retail price	£12,950 (early 1985)	£780.29	

Autocar, of course, had to treat the Naylor as a contemporary car, so wrote that:

> By current sports car standards the car is slow; certainly the low overall power output (77bhp at 5,180rpm) for the size of the engine, and unaerodynamic shape, limit the performance ... The engine note does not sound like a Morris Ital, but then again it does not sound like a traditional sports car either ... The light, responsive steering is ideal for round-town driving, but when travelling at speed it allows quite pronounced wandering as the wheel is only slightly moved...

All in all, it was not a favourable test, and my own impression was that the testers wondered whether or not they were having their legs pulled? That, too, must have been an impression gained by possible customers.

It wasn't long before the financial cracks began to show in the project. Although £360,000 had originally been raised, the TF1700 had already cost £100,000 to develop, setting up the factory had added to that, and national type approval had also been costly. Naylor therefore sought to raise an extra £250,000 in May 1985, targetting the Far East (Japan, in particular) for expansion – and even mentioned the Morgan marque as one of its sales 'conquest' targets.

By the end of 1985, the UK price had risen to £13,950. Naylor was seeking to appoint up to ten UK dealerships, and had already gained approval to sell cars in Japan, Germany, Belgium and Holland. Even so, only sixty-six cars were sold in the entire year and the company lost £400,000. The crash came in May 1986 when a receiver, Cork Gulley, was called in; within weeks a new company called Naylor Sports Cars Ltd, financed by Maurice Hutson, had paid £500,000 to buy the business and get the TF1700 back into production, with Mark Hutson (Maurice's son) running things from day to day.

Although there was optimistic talk about building four or five cars a week, and of using the new Rover M16 6-valve 2-litre engine, little more seems to have happened. Although Prime Minister Margaret Thatcher was persuaded to give the latest car a great photo opportunity outside 10 Downing Street, and the name was changed from 'Naylor' to 'Hutson', it never came back into prominence. There was also a kit-built version called the Mahcon TF, which also seems to have disappeared without trace.

What went wrong? Two things, I feel: one was that although it looked like an MG TF, quite simply it wasn't one. This, allied to the fact that in the 1980s a fully built-up Naylor/Hutson always cost a lot more than a fine-condition MG TF from the 1950s, meant that there was really no incentive to buy one!

Bloodied, but fortunately still in business, Alistair Naylor drew back into his entirely separate restoration and parts supply business. Many TFs have been rebuilt with bodyshells supplied from Yorkshire in recent years.

Appendix 3
EX175: T-Series Successor?

Everyone knows that it was the MGA which took over from the last of the TFs in 1955, but not everyone knows what came in between: the EX175. This fascinating one-off project bridged the gap, and has its own rather complicated story to tell. The fact is that the chassis was inspired from one direction, the body style from another, while the engine and running gear was modified from that of the TF1500!

As detailed in Chapter 6, the story really begins with George Phillips and his much modified TC-based car, which raced at Le Mans in 1949 and 1950. This car was always hampered by poor aerodynamics, but as Phillips was eager to continue in 1951, this time with a TD chassis, Syd Enever and the MG engineers agreed to design and build him a special all-enveloping aluminium two-seater bodyshell. This style, which carried MG's project code of EX172, took shape in the first months of 1951, and was really done without official sanction, being well hidden away from Nuffield bosses at Cowley so that it could not be cancelled before it was completed! Registered UMG 400, this car raced at Le Mans in 1951, but without success.

As already noted, although the style was beautiful, the seat was far too high because it had to be mounted on the existing TD chassis, and Phillips's head stuck way out into the slip-stream. Irritated by this, later in 1951 Syd Enever and the young Roy

Brocklehurst then spent time designing a brand-new chassis frame in which the side members were swept well outboard of the centre line, which allowed the passenger seats to be lowered considerably. The new frame was much more rigid than the TD's frame had ever been, for there was also a massive scuttle-bracing superstructure.

Although that chassis might have formed the basis of a race car, the formation of BMC at this time killed off any such notions (Len Lord was known for his trenchant anti-motor racing views – had he not closed down the Abingdon racing shop at a moment's notice in 1935?). Instead, and with John Thornley's tacit approval, Enever and his followers used the new frame as the basis of EX175, a prototype of what they hoped could be a new MG road car. For this project they devised a new body style which looked similar to EX172, but was different in almost every detail.

This time the bodyshell was intended for series production, and was built from pressed steel panels produced at the Morris Bodies branch in Coventry. It had doors on both sides, proper bumpers, windscreen and sidescreens – in other words, it was meant to be a roadworthy sports car in every way. Compared with the MGA style which finally appeared in 1955, the only real difference was that the TF-style engine made a bonnet bulge necessary: one wonders what would have been done to minimize this if BMC had approved the project?

Under the skin, the running gear of EX175 was pure MG TF1500, complete with 63bhp/1,466cc engine, and the well proven TF-style gearbox and back axle assemblies. Hindsight suggests that although this car would have been considerably faster than the last of the TF1500s, its top speed would still have been less than 95mph (153km/h) – and we know that MG dearly wanted to offer a 100mph (160km/h) maximum on its next range of cars. Although MG's various 'stage tuning' kits had already proved that the XPEG engine could produce more power and torque, it would not have been easy to have matched those figures in series production form.

Only one such car was completed, and in the autumn of 1952 it was shown to Len Lord. MG bosses hoped that he would approve it, and agree to it being committed to production, for by other BMC standards it would not have involved a great deal of capital investment. Unhappily, BMC's chairman turned it down, preferring to back another new sports car project, Donald Healey's Austin A90-engined Healey 100: not only would this use 2.6-litre Austin engines (of which there was a surplus), but it could be built at Longbridge.

What was not spelt out at the time, but became increasingly obvious in the months which followed, was that Len Lord had no intention of prolonging the life of the XPAG/XPEG engine and drive-line any longer than was necessary, as he wanted to

EX175, more popularly known as HMO 6, was designed and built in 1952 and therefore predated the TF, which would never have been developed if EX175 had approved for production. There was a completely new chassis, but the running gear was pure MG TD Mk II, though with an XPEG engine. Frozen out at the time because BMC's Len Lord favoured the Austin-Healey 100, EX175 would come back later, in 1954: it would be thoroughly re-engineered, and was the basis of the MGA sports car.

replace it with the new corporate B-Series hardware instead. EX175 was therefore sidelined until 1954 when, as every MG enthusiast knows, it was the inspiration for the hugely successful MGA which finally went on sale in 1955.

Especially when the MGA project was started, EX175 – registered HMO 6 – was a useful development car at Abingdon. I last saw it in 1956 when I first visited the Lockheed factory at Leamington Spa, but it was later scrapped.

Appendix 4
T-Series Performance

By investigating British and United States sources, I have been able to assemble accurate performance figures for all except the short-lived TB model.

As far as I can see, MG never loaned TBs to the British motoring press for road test during peacetime. In the last few days before the outbreak of war in 1939, The *Light Car & Cycle Car* were lent a TB Tickford but published no figures, while *The Autocar*'s H. S. Linfield borrowed a TB (registered CJB 59) in 1940, running it in from brand new, but never taking any performance figures.

The TD II, TD Mk II, TF1250 and TF1500 test figures are extracted from *Road & Track* of the USA, while the other tests were originally published in *The Autocar*.

	TA	TC	TD	TDII	TD Mark 2
Engine size/ bhp	1,292/ 50	1,250/ 54	1,250/ 54	1,250/ 54	1,250/ 60
Mean maximum speed, mph(km/h)	78(126)	75(121)	80(129)	79(127)	81(131)
Acceleration (sec)					
0–30mph(48km/h)	6.1	5.7	6.2	5.2	5.2
0–40mph(64km/h)	-	-	-	8.8	7.5
0–50mph(82km/h)	15.4	14.7	15.3	13.8	11.1
0–60mph(96km/h)	23.1	22.7	23.5	19.4	16.5
0–70mph(112km/h)	–	–	44.4	31.8	24.4
Standing 1/4-mile (sec)	-	-	-	21.3	20.8
Overall fuel consumption, mpg(l/100km)	- (9.3l/100km)	-	- (10.3l/100km)	30.4*	27.4*

Typical fuel consumption, mpg(l/100km)	27–29 (10.4–9.70)	28–34 (10–8.3)	27–33 (10.4–8.6)	-	-
Unladen weight, lb (kg)	1,935 (878)	1,811 (821)	2,009 (911)	2,005 (909)	2,015 (914)

	TF1250	TF1500
Engine size/ bhp	1,250/ 57	1,466/ 63
Mean maximum speed, mph(km/h)	80(129)	85(137)
Acceleration (sec)		
0–30mph(48km/h)	5.5	4.8
0–40mph(64km/h)	8.8	7.1
0–50mph(82km/h)	13.0	11.0
0–60mph(96kmp/h)	18.9	16.3
0–70mph(112km/h)	29.0	24.7
Standing 1/4 mile (sec)	21.6	20.7
Overall fuel consumption, mpg (l/100km)	25–28.7* (11.3–9.9)	-
Typical fuel consumption, mpg (l/100km)	-	-
Unladen weight, lb (kg)	2,020 (916)	2,015 (914)

* These are Imperial mpg figures, converted from the original US figures.

Road Test Figures Compared

In interpreting test figures, the unfortunate historian usually encounters problems. As an example, to show that different independent sources record different figures for cars provided for road test, here is a comparison between *The Autocar* and *The Motor* TDs, as 'figured' in 1950, 1952 and 1953:

	The Autocar	*The Motor*	*The Motor*	*The Autocar*
Car identity:	FMO 265	FMO 265	GRX 19	HMO 233
Test published:	20-1-50	22-2-50	8-10-52	15-5-53
Maximum speed (mph)	80	77	77	73.5
Acceleration (sec):				
0–30mph	6.2	5.5	4.5	6.3
0–50mph	15.3	13.5	12.2	15.6
0–60mph	23.5	21.3	18.2	23.9
0–70mph	44.4	N/A	29.5	39.6
Top gear acceleration (sec)				
10–30mph	12.5	11.5	9.9	11.7
30–50mph	12.9	12.7	12.5	12.6
Fuel consumption range (mpg)	27–33	26.3	26.7	25
Unladen weight (lb)	2,009	2,016	1,960	1,995

Statisticians would have a field day in rubbishing these comparisons, for there were several random variables:

** Tests were always carried out 'two-up'. In those days *The Autocar* used a fifth wheel speedometer, whereas *The Motor* corrected the car's own speedometer instead.

** Because *The Autocar* did not quote an 'as tested' weight in 1950, we do not know how this affected acceleration.

** *The Autocar* was presumably first to test FMO 265 in 1950, and clearly it had done more mileage, to 'loosen off', before *The Motor* tried it a few weeks later. This explains, perhaps, why it accelerated better (its 'as tested' weight, too, may have been less) ™ but it does not explain why it had a slower top speed !

** In 1952 *The Motor* was amazed that the latest car (still running on 'Pool' petrol) had such better acceleration than the original. That car, in fact, looks suspiciously quick...

** In 1953 *The Autocar*, in its usual understated way, wondered why the latest car was no quicker on the high-octane branded petrols which had been reintroduced in February 1953. The two-way recorded top speed, please note, was the worst of all four cars tested in these years.

Appendix 5
T-Series Production and Deliveries

Although Abingdon's chassis records for TA to TD models are no longer available, BMIHT and other sources have provided these figures for T-Series production:

Annual Production

Calendar year	TA	TB	TC	TD	TF 1250	TF 1500
1936	765					
1937	1,028					
1938	1,017					
1939	193	379				
Followed by a six-year break because of World War II.						
1945			81			
1946			1,675			
1947			2,346			
1948			3,085			
1949			2,813	98		
1950				4,767		
1951				7,451		
1952				10,838		
1953				6,510	1,635	
1954					4,565	1,951
1955						1,449
Total	3,003	379	10,000	29,664	6,600	3,400

From the same sources, it is also possible to assemble the figures for home market and export deliveries. It has not been possible, however, to quote accurate figures for the TA and TB models.

186

Total Deliveries

Model	Years built	Home market	Export North America	Export other	CKD/ chassis	Total
TA	1936–39					3,003
TB	1939					379
TC	1945–1949	3,408	2,001	4,497	94	10,000
TD	1949–1953	1,656	23,488	3,911	609	29,664
TF	1953–1955	1,057	6,235	2,221	87	9,600

* CKD = 'completely knocked down', which is industry-speak for cars exported in kits, for final assembly in other countries.

Total Abingdon Production

Note : These figures also include production of other MG models, and (from 1949) of Riley RM series models. I am sorry that a more detailed breakdown of 1930s figures is not available. Figures quoted for the 1930s are rounded up, while those quoted for 1955 include the first 1,003 MGA sports cars.

Calendar year	Home market	Export USA	Export other	CKD	Total
1930					1,850
1931					1,400
1932					2,400
1933					2,200
1934					2,100
1935					1,300
1936 [T-Series production began]					2,100
1937					2,900
1938					2,500
1939					1,900
1945	34		47		81
1946	1,001		638	36	1,675
1947	1,591	6	1,656	16	3,269
1948	584	1,493	1,985	114	4,176
1949	2,421	662	3,800	163	7,046
1950	2,630	2,825	4,429	546	10,430
1951	2,369	5,757	2,741	198	11,065
1952	2,575	9,901	1,108	85	13,669
1953	3,012	6,400	1,020	107	10,539
1954	5,276	4,218	3,326	155	12,975
1955	7,697	1,288	4,908	245	14,138